A'ūdhu billāhi minash-shaitānir-rajīm.
I seek refuge in God from the accursed satan.

Bismillāhir-Rahmānir-Rahīm.
In the name of God, the Most Compassionate, the Most Merciful.

Secrets
of the
Last Ant Man

M. R. Bawa Muhaiyaddeen ﴿رض﴾

Fellowship Press
Philadelphia, PA

This volume of *Secrets of the Last Ant Man* is unabridged and comes to these pages directly from the recorded words of M. R. Bawa Muhaiyaddeen ☮. Every effort has been made to keep the purity of his words intact. Nothing has been intentionally added, subtracted, or rearranged.

Library of Congress Control Number: 2019947571
Muhaiyaddeen, M. R. Bawa.
    Secrets of the Last Ant Man/
    M. R. Bawa Muhaiyaddeen ☮.
    Philadelphia, PA: Fellowship Press, 2020
    p. cm.
    Includes index.
    Trade paperback: 978-1-943388-48-6
    Hardcover: 978-1-943388-49-3

1. Allāh. 2. Sufism. 3. Islām. 4. Ant Man. 5. 'Ilm. 6. Muhammad ☮. 7. Qutb ☮. 8. Qur'ān. 9. Kalimah. 10. God. 11. Truth. 12. Faith. I. Title.

Copyright © 2020
by Bawa Muhaiyaddeen Fellowship
5820 Overbrook Avenue, Philadelphia, Pennsylvania 19131

All rights reserved. No portion of this document
may be reproduced in any manner
without written permission from the publisher.

Printed in the United States of America
by FELLOWSHIP PRESS
Bawa Muhaiyaddeen Fellowship
First Printing

Muhammad Raheem Bawa Muhaiyaddeen ﷺ

Contents

The Last Ant Man	1
The Secret of the Anthill	7
The Secret Place in the Jungle	23
The Secret of the Shaikh	33
The Secret of My Life	43
The Secret Book	67
The Secret of Direct Worship	87
M. R. Bawa Muhaiyaddeen ﷺ	111
Glossary	115
Index	123

The Last Ant Man
October 5, 1973

THE QUESTION (*addressed to the translator*) I don't know at this point whether the inner connection between Bawa and me is strong enough to be away from him—to keep that peacefulness, to see things clearly. I don't know about that.

BAWA MUHAIYADDEEN☺ It is not strong enough, that is true.

THE WOMAN WHO ASKED THE QUESTION What do I do?

BAWA MUHAIYADDEEN☺ You have to make the connection stronger. You have planted the seedling. Now you have to let it grow a strong root. Then it will become a tree. You planted it and now you have to water it until it can draw its own water. Until then, it will be a little unsteady. It will get its own water when the right root grows down. Until then, you have to water and care for the seedling. After it takes root, it will draw in what it needs by itself.

THE WOMAN WHO ASKED THE QUESTION But will that be possible if I am away from him? That's what I'm asking.

SECRETS OF THE LAST ANT MAN

BAWA MUHAIYADDEEN ☮ You have to be strong.

THE WOMAN WHO ASKED THE QUESTION I'm not very strong.

BAWA MUHAIYADDEEN ☮ You need to make the effort. I will tell you one true thing.

In the world, there is an Ant Man. He is the last one. For thirteen hundred years he has been the last Ant Man in the world. You will not be able to find another. That is the truth. Thus, if you have the determination, hold on to him. His agreement is that he will be here for a little while longer, and then he will have to disappear. After that, the destruction of the world will come—the wars and the destruction will come.

He is the last man, the last Ant Man for his time, a very subtle man. If you can make the effort, you must endeavor to hold on to him. There has been no Ant Man like this Ant Man of the last thirteen hundred years. No one has seen such a thing. It is a secret. Make the effort to hold on to him. You must hold on to him in a very subtle way. It is your responsibility.

The rain will keep falling. It is your responsibility to catch the water and preserve it. It is your responsibility to find it and pour it onto your seedling. It is your responsibility until the seedling can draw its own water from the ground. After that, it is the seedling's responsibility.

It is not the rain's responsibility. The rain is doing its duty by raining.

However, not everyone can come to that point. Only one or two out of ten million will come. It is very difficult. That is how it is. It is your responsibility.

The other day when you were in New York, you were with two people, and you said some things. I heard a little of it.

THE WOMAN WHO ASKED THE QUESTION Which specific thing is he speaking of?

BAWA MUHAIYADDEEN ☮ I am not far away. I have the ears to hear you. I have the eyes to see you. As soon as I hear the sound, I look to see where my child is going and what she is doing.

If this tiny Ant Man's ears can hear like that, how much more my God who sees everything can see and hear! He has such vast ears. Therefore, you must put your faith in God. The Ant Man has a bit of wisdom—endeavor to obtain it. That is what will understand the truth. Keep studying it.

It is not as it is said to be. It depends upon your strength.

You spoke of three sections and I heard the three sections. The two people were on one side and you were on the other. I heard you speaking.

THE WOMAN WHO ASKED THE QUESTION Was that okay?

BAWA MUHAIYADDEEN ☮ I cannot say it was right. I will say it is right when you become right. If there are three diverging branches on the tree, we cannot say there is one branch. If there are three stars, we cannot say there is one star. There is one star only if there actually is one star.

Now there is one tree with three branches. Make the three branches one.

That will be very strong.

The Secret of the Anthill
July 31, 1973

All of you—Anne, June, Rodger Tambi, Dick Tambi, Bob Tambi, Moon Pillay, Secretary Pillay, Hanal Tambi, John Tambi, and Salihu Tambi—are very, very great people, great in wisdom and education. There are many, many great people in America. Everyone is a great person, educated in science and everything else.

But I[1] am a small person.

I do not even know whether to call myself a human being. I do not know whether to call myself a man or an animal. I do not know whether to call myself a bird. I do not know whether to call myself a snake or an insect. I am a man smaller than an ant, a being smaller than an ant.

I have no education. I do not know how to study. I have no title. I do not know English. I do not know how to read Tamil. I do not know the scriptures. I have no *gnānam*, no wisdom, no money, no wealth, no house, or property. I have no *gnānam*, no wisdom, no knowledge. I do not know who God is.

---

1   "I"   Bawa Muhaiyaddeen ☺ rarely used the word "I." These phrases are expressed in Tamil without the "I" pronoun, and simply indicated in the verb. In English, unfortunately, we are forced to use the "I" for clarity.

I have never seen a human being. I do not know what that is. I have not seen a human being. I have not seen God. I have not seen any titles or honors. I do not know what the world is. I do not know what titles are. I have no knowledge of any books of *gnānam* or any literature of *gnānam*.

I am a small thing, a small ant, who knows none of these things—a tiny ant—so I do not know any wisdom. I do not know any art. I have not studied ragas nor do I know any music.

I do not know music. I do not know how to drive a car or anything else. I do not have wings to fly in the sky. I do not have horns to dig myself a hole in the earth. I have no place in which to hide. I have no house in which to live.

This is how I exist in God's creation as a very, very, very, very tiny man in the world. I am a little Ant Man.

I do not know religion. I do not know the way. I do not know the scriptures. I do not know caste. I have not learned what caste is. I have not studied it. I have not studied what worship is.

We do not have any worship titles or God titles. We do not have a swami title, an *'ālim* title, a pope title, a bishop title, a minister title, a *lebbay* title, a *pūjāri* title, a brahmin title, a preacher title, a guru title, a teacher title, a title for magic tricks, a title for mantras, a title for stringing flowers for the temple, a title for doing *pūjās*, a title for summoning a god, a title for seeing gods—for seeing the four hundred trillion gods. We do not have a title for summoning them.

I have not studied. I am very small, smaller than an ant. I am a little Ant Man beside whom even the ants look enormous. I do not know very much of anything. I am a very discarded man.

I do not have an answer for any of the questions you ask me.

> *Teaching ignorant people*
> *about* gnānam *and books of revelation*
> *will ruin even a domestic life.*[2]

God has said this and people of wisdom have sung that song. I am not God, nor am I a man of wisdom, nor am I someone who has finished learning wisdom, nor am I someone who has finished learning *gnānam*, nor am I someone who has finished learning about God. I have not seen Him or known Him.

Great wise men, great *gnānis*, have told us:

> *Teaching ignorant people*
> *about* gnānam *and books of revelation*
> *will ruin even a domestic life.*

When God's secret falls into the hands of these monkeys who do not know its splendor, it is similar to what happens to a flower garland in the hands of a monkey. If the monkeys say, "I am God! You are God!" that is what happens. This is their title in the world.

I do not know how to take on a title because I did not learn that. Nor do I understand it.

Can I study that? How can a little ant study? I am a little ant, an Ant Man. I cannot study. Such a small being cannot study. How did I come to visit America? I crawled here. I simply kept crawling and arrived here.

I came here in order to study, but I did not understand the lessons everyone was speaking of. They did not use ant language. All the lessons were taught in great, great languages.

I could not find any lessons in ant language.

Everyone had huge titles: swami titles, *pūjāri* titles, titles for seeing God, titles for seeing the world, titles for science,

---

2   domestic life   This is the mundane level of life, where material wealth and earning a living take precedence over the search for truth.

titles for ignorance, titles for love, titles for manias, titles for music, a title for having come as a god, a guru title, an enmity title, a firewood title.³ They all exist here.

I never found the language we came here to study. I never found a language suitable for an ant, for a tiny man. I could not study it. I am in America just blinking my eyes, unable to learn. My eyes do not see, my ears do not hear, my tongue does not speak. I am a very, very tiny man.

What can I do? I have no billboard, no position, no title. What should I do, children?

The tiny man *is* a little older than you. But what can I do? I do not know the language. I do not understand what to do. I have no *gnānam*, no wisdom. I do not know how to become a human being. I have been worried because I have no title, because I have not studied at a university or anywhere else.

The *pūjāris*, the *āchāris*, the swamis, and the gods have all come here to America. The gods all came to America and started wearing the *original God* as a hat! Therefore, what can we say, children?

Do whatever you want.

I came here in order to learn. If you know something, teach me. I do not understand education. Very, very great scholars have come into the world. There are so many in America—a thousand gurus have come. I do not know any gurus who would teach a small ant. However, the gurus, the titles, and the honors have come to the world as gods. Thus, if you know something, teach me a little.

I crawled and crawled and came to this country. Now I need to crawl back. All I am is an ant, a tiny ant. This is how it is in our history.

However, if you would like to know some ant language, I

---

3 guru, enmity, firewood   *Guru, veruppu, virahu*; Bawa Muhaiyaddeen ☙ is using these words as a humorous rhyming device, equating the first word with the subsequent rhyming words.

know a little. If you would like to learn the language spoken by a tiny ant, I can teach you.

To learn, you have to follow the path traveled by the ants and pass through a small hole in the ground. If you come like that and keep going, you can study ant language and learn about our lineage, and the events in the ant colony. For that, you have to go through the small hole. If you come inside to learn ant language, you will understand.

Huge, huge languages and the huge, huge swami titles cannot fit through the hole. There would be great difficulties. It is only an ant trail. Elephants, big men, gods, people with god titles, and any who want to bring along their *'ālim* titles, their world titles, their titles for claiming to have seen God face-to-face, their titles for claiming to have seen the swami face-to-face, their *gnāna* titles, boat titles, ship titles, or plane titles cannot enter. It is too difficult. They would get stuck and have to die.

It is only if you creep in like an ant that you can understand some of the secrets of the anthill. If you slowly keep crawling and transforming yourself into a tiny ant, you can enter the colony. The anthill is filled with secrets.

There is a saying:

Only the ant knows the secrets of the anthill.

Therefore, if you want to understand the house built by the ant, you have to enter the anthill as an ant.

Only a white ant, a termite, can know the house built by the termites. Only a termite can build a termite house and understand it. No one can build a house like a termite builds under the ground. It is a great secret.

Sometimes a mongoose takes over the termite mound. Sometimes snakes live there. Sometimes rats live there. Snakes, mongooses, rats, lizards, centipedes, and scorpions kill and eat each other as they try to take over those mounds.

They try to drive out the termites and say, "This is my house!"

The snake says, "This is my house!" Then the mongoose goes after the snake—the mongoose and the snake are enemies. They say, "This is my house!" The lizard who goes to catch and eat the ants says, "*Ah*! This is my house!" The rat who goes there to eat all who have died within says, "This is my house!" The dog who goes to eat the rat, says, "This is my house!" The dog's keeper says, "All of them are food for us!"

Only the termite knows the secret rooms in the secret house built by the termites. That is their experience. The other creatures go to take over the mound, claiming it for themselves, saying, "I! My house!" fighting over it and trying to take possession of it.

That is how the worldly titles and the swami titles take over the creation-house built with such subtlety by God.

They try to take over God's secret, His mystery, the wonders of His creation, the exquisite wonder of how He creates, protects, and sustains; His explanations of compassion and love; His three thousand blessings; His grace, His generosity, His mercy; the peacefulness, patience, tolerance, and tranquility that comprise His justice; how He loves others and shows them affection through His actions, deeds, and conduct; and how His nature is such that even if your mother and father forget you, He will never forget you.

He is the One who is the Great Almighty One who protects His creations and feeds them, sustains them, watches over them, and then calls them back unto Himself. The house He has built—the creation-house—contains man's greatness and his abilities, God's power, the greatness in the creations, the wonders within them, the wonder in what lies beyond those creations, along with the explanations and truth of the celestial beings, the messengers, the *ambiyā'*, and the *aqtāb* who tell us there is nothing equal to God.

Using the titles and honors of the world, the demons, the

The Secret of the Anthill

titled snakes, and the honorable mongooses say, "I," the demonic giants say, "mine," the demonic forces say, "my house," the evil, demonic satans say, "This house is mine! I am God!" and try to take over the marvelous thing that is the house God has built.

Saying, "I! I have descended from the skies! I have seen God! I am God! God is with me, look over here, look over there, look at this magic, this mantra, this trick! Look outside. Look over there at the light. Look over there at the stars. Look at that show, look at that guru, look at what is hidden there, look at the darkness! Look at me over there, look at you over there, look at love over there, look at lust over there, look at the house in which they are all mixed together!" They meet about these issues and get their titles, but they cannot enter the anthill.

You must avoid all of them. You must become an ant and discover the secret of the ant—the house built by the termites.

You must discover God's secret. Who is He? What sort of wonder is He? What shape does He have? What form does He have? Does He have children? Does He have a wife? Does He have a house? Does He have property? Does He have a shadow?

No. This wonder, this house that God has built, exists in every creation. These demons, these titled monkey troops try to enter His secret mystery and live there. The lizards try to live there. The mongoose, the rat, the snake, the dog, the cat, the centipede, the scorpion, and the tarantula try to break into it saying, "*Ai!* This is my house! I am God!"

But they cannot enter.

Therefore, leave all those things behind. If you want to understand the house God has built, you have to understand that He is a Power, a Light, without form or self-image. It is the Light that has to enter the secret and look at it. That is what the Light will understand.

That is the language of the tiny ant, the language of the tiny man who is smaller than an ant. If we want to see the house God has built, children, that is how we have to study the language. If we study like that, it will be really good.

It is a good language.

With it, you can escape from all the atom bombs. If you can discover how to crawl into the earth, you can escape from the atomic weapons they are soon going to deploy, and the wars, the conflicts, the bombs, the explosives. If you stay in the anthill, they cannot affect you.

If you obtain a title, the atom bombs outside will fall on you. Illnesses, diseases, terrible cancers, karmic diseases, the diseases of hell, diseases like lions, diseases like tigers—demonic, man-eating diseases will come from the atom bombs, from the air, the fire, the water, the earth, the sky, everywhere. There will be danger everywhere you turn and you will be trapped.

Thus, if you want to escape from any kind of bomb, you must realize that only the termite can build a termite house and understand its secrets.

It builds with its mouth. This is a house built of a mixture of water and earth from which all its separate elements have been extracted. The termite extracts the elements as it builds: the gold is separate, the iron is separate, the copper is separate. There is a part used for making the food, a part used for making the house. You cannot be like those other creatures if you are going to build an essence-house like this. If you build the house, you will learn the language.

Yes. That is the language.

The language in America is the language of a thousand gurus and swami titles. This is not it. That is the language of a tiny ant. If you want to learn ant language, you have to know it is a subtle language. You have to be able to pass through a tiny hole in the ground like an ant.

The Secret of the Anthill

So children, if you want to do that, there is an ant language school—but no people. There is a school, but there are no people in it.

At the school, there is a certain kind of sound, a "*shh, chku, chku, chku, chku,*" sound. Where does the sound come from? It has no form. You will hear the sound, "*Coo, coo, coo, coo.*" You cannot tell where it is coming from. The sound has a Light, but not a form. "*Hoo, hoo, hoo,*" the sound will call. Where is it coming from? There is only the resonance—we cannot see any people. "*Ah, oo,*" comes the sound. We cannot tell which *vīna* it comes from. The sound contains so many parts, so many ragas! We cannot see any people. The sound has power. There is much, much, much more like that.

The school does exist. There are no people. The lessons are all in shorthand. The song it sings must be taken down in shorthand and then typed. The shorthand can later be examined in discrete parts. All the sounds must be recorded. Then, they must be typed—*tak, tak, tak, tak*—with Pērarivu, the subtle seventh level of wisdom. After the typing is complete, the document must be examined in parts. Then it will be understood. Then we can learn that particular raga. Then we can read the music.

In this school, there are many, many, many schools. And there is a test to be taken where all the schools come together in one section. This is how you have to study in that school. There is a tremendous reverberating sound. There are cooing, whirring, and buzzing sounds. Sounds of prayer. There are many, many sounds. This is how to learn the secrets of the Ant—and God.

Do you understand? Secretary? Moon? Dr. Tambi? Anne? Baby? Bob? Hanal Tambi? Jean? June? Rabia? Ayeshamma? All the children. This is an explanation for each of the thousand children. Think about it. This is how it is.

Yes? This is how it is. You cannot do it if you have a title for closing your eyes and standing on your head. You cannot do it by walking on your hands. You cannot do it even if you raise your buttocks and walk on your back. You cannot get through the entrance like that. You can only enter it if you become an ant. This is God's secret.

Early morning. I give the children many, many humble greetings.

> *The translator tells Bawa Muhaiyaddeen☉ about something someone had mentioned earlier.*

BAWA MUHAIYADDEEN☉ He came here, but he left. Those people require titles. They need the sun and the moon. They need "the light." They need mantras. They need magic. They need to say, *om, nam, nee, oom.*

We do not have titles. I am a tiny man, an Ant Man. It is difficult. This may happen to you too, in future, future times. Pay no attention to titles. Only an ant knows the secrets of the anthill. Only a termite knows the secrets of the termite mound—how to build a building like that.

Similarly, only God knows God's secret. And similarly, we must take the appropriate form if we want to discover the secret. You should not look at titles, honors, accolades, or celebrity. If you look at those things, you will not be able to creep into the anthill. You will have to die from the atom bombs. *Ai?* You will die from the storms and the hurricanes.

Titles are for amassing money in business. They are not for reaching God. Understand this.

It is not about whirling around in a dance and saying "*Al-hamdu lillāh*. I die, die, die, die, die."

Ahamed Muhaiyaddeen? The time for the ABCD lesson is over.

That is why I do not need a history. In every country, they said to me, "O Swami, tell us your history. O Guru Bawangal," they said, offering me many, many titles with an incredible amount of noise.

They sang hymns of praise while they tried to present raja titles to the Ant Man. They offered him king jobs in many countries. "No," I said in those countries.

They tried to marry me to princesses. *Hmn.* They tried to give me a *pulavar* title. *Hmn.* A swami title. *Hmn. Apapapapā!* How many they tried to give me! That is why they asked for histories. They tried to make me an *'ālim*, a brahmin." *Hmn,* I cannot enter into those things. I can only enter the anthill.

Danger could come to you from the storms and the hurricanes that will have to come to pass, from the tidal waves, the fires, and the storms that will come to the world along with rain, floods, volcanoes, earthquakes, the poison mixed with thunder that will fall from the skies, and the clouds of toxic vapor. If you are big at that time, you will be trapped by the danger. You will not be able to fully enter the anthill. You will be too big, and you will die.

Thus, to know God, to enter the anthill, you do not need titles, you do not need money, you do not need a country, you do not need a nation, you do not need the "I am God" attitude. You must go as "I am nothing." For those who claim to have seen God, there is an ancient saying: "Even no one in the heavens has seen God."

God told Moses ☮ on Mount Sinai, "He who has seen Me will not survive. He will not survive—he will die. The 'I' will die. He who has seen Me will not survive in the world. The 'I' will die and he will be nothing." God spoke like that to every *nabī*, every prophet.

That is the secret. No one has seen God. Has anyone seen God? No. Even Moses ☮ did not see God. He just heard the sound. Muhammad ☪ did not see God. He saw himself in the resplendence, the *wahy*, the revelation. Everyone who met God saw only the resplendence and then saw themselves within the resplendence. This is how the *ambiyā'* and the heavenly messengers brought the secrets. We have to understand them.

There is very, very much education in America. It is only in wisdom that they are a little—they do not know how to proceed as small beings in order to understand. They do not know how to proceed like tiny ants in order to understand the secrets of the ants or the anthill.

Aiyō! Some people lay hands on the bodies of others to heal them. Some people lay hands on their eyes to heal them. Some people claim to have transformed themselves into God. Some people claim to be God. "This is the guru, that is the firewood,"[4] and so forth. That is the wonder.

If you wished to write about wonders and you were to begin writing about the gurus of America—about the gurus and about devotion—you could not finish writing about them even if you kept writing until the end of the world.

If you looked at it with the truth, like an ant, you would have to smile. You would have to smile at the huge forms your brothers and sisters have taken, and cry because those huge forms are going to die in the fire. When you look at the swamis, the gurus, their people, and their titles, you would have to cry, "They are going to die in the fire, in the storms, the floods, the hurricanes. Look at these forms, *appā, aiyō*! What a shame!"

This is a way to do business, a business that needs no capital investment, a business that can be profitably conducted in a place where many fools gather.

There is the sound of a cicada in the background.

The cicada is calling the rain.

---

4   This is the guru, that is the firewood   *Itu guru, atu veruhu*; Bawa Muhaiyaddeen ☺ is using these words as a humorous rhyming device to compare a guru with firewood (for hell).

Then there is the sound of a baby fussing. Bawa Muhaiyaddeen☮ speaks to the baby:

What kind of noise are *you* making? What is it? The little ones speak a type of ant language. What kind of creature is making the noise? It is a baby-bug. It too is little, and it too crawls on the ground.

The cicada roams in moist places. When the moisture dries up, the cicadas think of God and make that noise. When they make that sound, it is a sign of the coming of the rains.

The baby suddenly makes a loud noise and Bawa Muhaiyaddeen☮ speaks to it again.

Rain? The rain is coming.

There is also a bird that is like an eagle. It is white. We can see them flying in the sky above the ashram. It is a type of eagle, called a *nīr-kanni*. That bird circles in the sky, three, four, five thousand feet high, and makes a certain cry that has the power to make the clouds come down.

The way this occurs is that ice and water contain the energies of the demons. If you set off an explosion on ice, the ice will begin to thunder. The demonic energy will make a loud "*aagh*!" noise. This is a secret.

In places where there is ice in mountainous areas, the thundering, booming noise you hear then is a demon, a water-demon. The ice contains the essence of the water-demon. You can hear a thundering crack and a "*shhk*," like a lightning bolt. If you set a stick of dynamite or place a source of heat there on the ice, the demon's energy will leave with a "*shhk*" sound. When it leaves, it can strike and kill people. When one part breaks off, others will be broken too, and there can be an avalanche.

So when the demon-clouds hear the sound of that bird, they will be startled and release the rain. Rain will fall from those clouds. The cry of the bird and the call of the cicada are signs of coming rain. The cicada made that chirring sound for a little while.

There are many similar parts and things in your body. The signs are all there. Secretary.

That child, that little baby is a good baby. Hi! Baby! Baby!

The Secret Place in the Jungle
July 31, 1972

There was a place about eighteen miles from Kataragama where I used to stay when I lived in the jungle. I had a bed to sleep in, and everything else I needed. In the jungle, eighteen miles from Kataragama, I had a bed and a pillow made of stone in the river.

About a mile into the deep jungle, there was a level area with trees. The river flowed around it. There were three large stones: a stone for me, and two stones for two more people, lower down. There were also some smaller stones upon which I could sit, and stones upon which I could place my feet.

ARABY (NOORUL AMEENA MACAN-MARKAR) Who, Bawangal, were the two other people?

BAWA MUHAIYADDEEN ☺ Just people. Men. There was an *ūnjal* tree, a tree that moved in the wind like a swing where I could sit and swing peacefully in the branches. There was water, there were rocks. The tree was on this side of them.

Eighteen of us went to that place one day. I showed it to Pariari and the others who came with us. The bed where I slept and the place where I sang songs had been a great, great secret. Pariari, the Clarkan who is gone, Malayala Muttaiyya, the manager, Kumaraswami Tambi, the man who brought milk the other day, the overseer, Kandaiyya, and Sundarasēran Pillay were among those who saw it.

We went to that place, and when we got there, old memories came flooding back to me. I thought, "This is an opportunity to escape from you—it would be so good if I could just stay here."

They saw many secrets in that place. They saw many people coming and going. However, let's let that be for now.

One day, when I was sitting in that place, there were a lot of monkeys. The reason for this is that the first people to come to Lanka-puri were monkeys. Ravanan came after Kubēran. The *asūras* came after Ravanan and seventy battalions of monkeys came with Rama. *Rākshidas, kubēras,* and *asūras*—evil giants, immensely wealthy, malevolent dwarves, and hideous demons—lived here first. Then Sita came with Ravanan and then Rama with seventy battalions of monkeys.

Therefore, Lanka-puri is a monkey kingdom, because the monkeys were here first! Here people are in the minority. One Rama—one human being—came with seventy battalions of monkeys. Thus, there are many more monkeys here than people. This is most certainly a monkey kingdom. Three-quarters of them are monkeys, people are in the minority. The monkeys came first, long ago.

So there I was sitting next to the tree in the middle of the river. If you go another eighteen miles in the other direction, this river is the river that meets the Valliammai river. I was in the middle of this river that day.

There was a rock and a group of beautiful trees. Between the trees were rocks around which water flowed. The rock in the middle of the river could be reached by using the other rocks as stepping-stones. When I slept there, how wonderfully cool it was. It was easy to stay there and meditate. There were trees growing all around, beautiful shade trees bending low above me. Because of the coolness, because of the water flowing all around, I could stay on the rock for eight days, ten days, twenty days. It was very beautiful. Even when the floods came, they would not take me, they just went by. There I sat, and there I rested. It was very beautiful. The fish jumped. The animals called. It was very good. There were fish everywhere, so many of them.

I rested there that day, reclining on the rock, lying on my side with my head propped up in my hand. The way the water flowed and how the breeze blew made it chilly, and I had to wear a shirt.

While I was resting like that, a leopard had appeared on the bank of the river and was climbing down to the water.

There were multitudes of monkeys. As soon as they saw the leopard, the monkeys on both sides of the river began to shriek, "*Kai, pooey! Kuy, kai, kuy!*" The noise was indescribable. It was a large leopard.

I opened my eyes wondering why the monkeys were making so much noise. I had been there for seven days. This was the seventh. When I looked around I saw that the monkeys were making the noise because of the leopard.

The leopard was running down the embankment to the sand by the shore. The monkeys were screeching, and I was sitting on the rock watching.

When the leopard stepped onto the sand, about five or six hundred monkeys began to screech. The leopard sank into the wet sand. It stood there for a moment and then fell over. The monkeys on both banks were shrieking. There was a *tāttān*-monkey, a grandfather-monkey, in a tree next to the river, a *panīchay* tree full of fruit. After some time had passed, the monkeys began to pick the fruit and throw it at the leopard. They each picked off a fruit and threw it.

DR. AJWAD What is a *tāttān*-monkey?

BAWA MUHAIYADDEEN ☺ The *tāttān*-monkey was the fat one. He had climbed down a little lower in the tree than the rest of them. They were all throwing the *panīchay* fruit at the leopard. It seemed to be lying there dead.

I thought, *The leopard was so healthy when it arrived at the riverbank, what kind of disease could it have caught that would kill it so suddenly?*

The leopard was about as far from me as we are now from the temple on the corner. It was lying in the sand. The monkeys threw so many fruits at it, but it did not open its eyes or get up. "*Kaai, poo!*" screeched the monkeys until eventually all of them came to sit in the *panīchay* fruit tree. They screeched loudly.

The monkeys that had scattered when they saw the leopard now gradually began to descend from branch to branch, hooting and screeching. The grandfather-monkey quickly jumped to the ground. He went to sit a little closer to the leopard, watching it carefully. He picked up sand and a rock and threw it at the leopard. It did not move.

Gradually, all the other monkeys climbed down, one after the other. They formed a majority, edging closer and closer to the leopard. The beach was now in possession of the monkeys.

The leopard was motionless. One of the monkeys moved two feet closer to the leopard, pelting it with sand, leaping away, and watching for a reaction. Then another pelted it with sand, leaped away, and watched for a reaction. The leopard lay there as if it were dead. The grandfather-monkey crept very close to the leopard who was lying completely still with its tail stretched out. The grandfather-monkey pulled at the tail and quickly pivoted on one leg, jumping out of the way. The leopard did not say a thing.

The Secret Place in the Jungle

The monkeys all gradually came down out of the tree. One monkey ran towards the leopard, slapped its belly and ran away. Another one came from another direction and slapped its back. Another one came and slapped it in another place. They were all making that noise, all gathered together, jumping here, jumping there, striking him in one place or another. One pulled his ear and quickly leaped away. The leopard lay in perfect silence.

They all joined together, making the *kai, pooey* noise, pulling and scratching at it, but the leopard did not react. All of them came to stand around it. One of them pulled at the hair on its back. This activity continued for an hour. By the time they had finished, they surrounded the leopard. There were five or six hundred monkeys surrounding it, and they were so close that the leopard was not visible at all.

I stood up and watched. I stood on the rock, but I still could not see the leopard. Suddenly, the leopard exploded out of the group striking a blow here and a blow there. Two monkeys fell to the ground. The rest of them screeched and hooted as they ran away. Only two monkeys were left on the beach. The leopard ripped them apart with one blow and they died in a second. They lay on the ground, looking as if they were grinning.

The leopard tore open the bellies of both monkeys and ate their livers. Their bodies were completely torn open. It bit into the tail of one of the monkeys and then the other, and dragged them off, grasping both tails in its jaws. It dragged away both of them by their tails.

ARABY (NOORUL AMEENA MACAN-MARKAR) What did the other monkeys do?

BAWA MUHAIYADDEEN ☻ They vanished high into the treetops, screaming *kai-chee-poo-chee*. There was not even a baby left on the beach. The grandfather-monkey was one of those killed. He had been caught. The leopard dragged the two dead monkeys along the shore of the river and out of sight.

After it was over and I went to take a closer look, it seemed as if the sand had been plowed up! There was a crooked tree growing a little way from there, a tree like a *maruda* tree, a jujube, growing wild. The two monkeys hung from it on a branch just above head height, neatly folded over the bough as if asleep. The leopard had stashed them there to eat later.

That is how someone who knows the truth of God will be when he comes to the world. He will be silent. What will the monkeys do? The monkeys will pounce on him: *Oof! Gick!* They will scratch at him. *Ick!* They will pull on him. *Ip!* They will bite him. They will pelt him with sand. The monkeys will all make a terrible commotion, ridiculing him. *Ee! Ai!* They will pull on his tail, his ears, his whiskers. He will wait through all of it, through so many blows and kicks.

But when the time comes, he will take one breath, tear open the bellies of the monkeys, and eat them. The time will come. He is waiting. Sometimes this country treats him like the monkeys were treating the leopard.

I sat there, looking at what had happened to the monkeys, thinking, *This is the way it is. This is what the monkeys do to the slaves of God. This is what they have done to us in so many places. This is a true story. God has given it to us and placed it in front of our eyes. He is watching us.*

There is no difference between these monkeys and those monkeys. It is all monkey mischief. The human monkeys do this and the animal monkeys do this. That is what I was thinking to myself.

When I compare animal and human monkeys as I look at the world, the other monkeys and the monkey-mind monkeys are completely alike. I have seen and experienced this. There is no difference between them. Those are monkeys with tails, these are monkeys without tails. They both engage in the same mischief.

If a person is minding his own business, they scratch at him a little, grinning, *Ee!* They throw something at him, and then they throw something else at him. They ridicule him. They pull at his whiskers. They pull at his legs. They pull at his tail.

There are two species of monkeys like this—seventy battalions. Those were the monkeys—a thousand eight kinds of monkeys—that got here first, to Lanka-puri, and that is what those monkeys will do. But one day, that slave of God will rise up like the leopard and have to strike them. One day.

This is the story of what I saw and experienced. It was something I experienced. How patient the leopard was.

The man is doing his work, but the monkeys think the leopard has died. Why won't they let it be? Why do the monkeys create the mischief?

That is how it is. That is how I am lying here.

The Secret of the Shaikh
November 17, 1973

BAWA MUHAIYADDEEN ☺ Shaikh Hammad ☺ is a secret in the *dunyā*.

TRANSLATOR Shaikh Hammad ☺ was the Master of the Qutb ☺, and the Qutb ☺ was also the Master of Shaikh Hammad ☺.

BAWA MUHAIYADDEEN ☺ When Hammad ☺ came to the *dunyā*, the world, he was the Qutb's Shaikh. In the *akhirah*, the kingdom of God, the Qutb ☺ was Hammad's Shaikh.

This name [Hammad] just came to my lips and I said it immediately. It is a good name, a name of *daulat*, great wealth. Hammad is the name of the Shaikh of the Qutbiyyah of the fifty-first generation [after the Rasūl ☺]. Hammad ☺ was the Qutb's Shaikh the ninety-ninth time he came. Hammad Shaikh ☺ is not an easy name.

Hammad ☺ came for spiritual *īmān*. He was also the Shaikh to Qutb Khawajah ☺ of Ajmer.

It is said that he who has not been touched by the foot of the Qutb ☺ will never be a *walī*, a saint, that no one can obtain the state of sainthood in any other way.

When we speak of the Qutbiyyah, we are speaking of that which appeared at the very beginning, the vibration. The Qutbiyyah comes in a vibration. It is not something that comes from anything in the *dunyā*. It comes from within—it emerges from within *īmān*. It is called Qutbiyyah.

What comes from the Qutb☺ is wisdom. What comes from the outside comes from the mind as book knowledge and similar things.

The Qutbiyyah is something that comes directly from wisdom as a vibration that has a power, an *ōsay*—a compelling vocal sound that arrives as a summons. The *ōsay* comes when the power is tapped. The *ōsay* comes from the place that is struck by the vibration. There is no *ōsay* in places struck by things such as book knowledge. There is no *ōsay* in that which moves through the intellect.

That is why the Qutbiyyah is on the other side and why it is called wisdom. It is something else, a vibration. It is different.

We still do not understand *īmān*. We do not understand what it means. It is said, "He who understands *īmān* was a *sīmān*—a person of immense wealth—in the *awwal*, the beginning." He who understands *īmān* is a person of limitless wealth. Such a person will have the wealth of *īmān* in the *ākhirah* and in the *dunyā*.

We do not understand *īmān*.

That is why God has said, "*Yā* Muhammad, tell them to accept *īmān*, to accept faith, determination, and certitude! Give *īmān* to your *ummah*, your community." That is *īmān*.

After God gave him those words, He said to him, "He who has *īmān* is a *sīmān*." To explain the power within *īmān*, He told him about Īmān-Islām, its limitlessness. *Īmān* is Islām, it is purity. Islām is limitless, abundant purity. He who has *īmān* is an immensely wealthy person.

Thus, *īmān* is Islām, it is purity. The wealth that God has is limitlessly abundant. That is what has been said. That is the explanation.

Without *īmān*, Islām does not exist. He who does not know the meaning of *īmān* will always be in want. He who is in want will not have *īmān*. He who has *īmān* is completely content with what he has. He is the *sīmān*, Allāh's *sīmān*.

There is no *īmān* where limitless abundance is not embraced, limitless abundance. *Īmān* means he lacks nothing—he lacks nothing whatsoever. He has accepted Allāh with firm determination. He has accepted Allāh as Allāh and thus he lacks nothing.

He has no self, so he has no want. He has accepted Allāh. He has no joy, no sorrow, no want, no hunger, no aging, no death. He has accepted *īmān*.

That is Īmān-Islām. Only he who understands *īmān* is able to become a Muslim.

What people talk about is not Islām. It is not Islām—it is an example and does not belong to *īmān*. It is an example, a tree through the branches of which *īmān* is revealed. It is like showing someone the location of the moon, the crescent moon, through the branches of a tree. It is like saying, "Look over there, below that branch, under that cloud. Look over there." It is an example, a way, to show someone the moon.

We must go deep inside. We can see *īmān* only if we go inside. *Īmān* is not a simple matter. The vibration of that which is called the Qutbiyyah is generated through *īmān*.

We say, "Sufi, Sufi, Sufism, Sufi, Sufism!" Sufis are sometimes referred to as *gnānis*—however, that is a definition we would have to laugh at.

Sufism means to learn. Sufi means *odukkam*—cessation, absolute disappearance. Everything is finished. Everything has stopped. It means *maunam*, silence. There is no sound. There is nothing.

It means what was there before is no longer there—it has

ceased to exist. The meaning is different, the interpretation is different, the behavior is different. It is no easy matter.

Sufi is the last word.

It exists beyond the Ten Commandments. It is the path that lies beyond the ten sins, beyond the ten openings of the body. The Ten Commandments are for the ten openings. The ten openings have to be closed. The visions seen by the eyes, the visions seen by all ten openings have to disappear. The place where everything that comes and goes through the ten openings is brought to a halt is called Sufism.

It is not a dance—there is no dance, no art, no song. There is no "I" to do those things.

Those things are all part of the *sharī'ah*. *Sharī'ah* is an Arabic word. It is easy to make noise in the *sharī'ah*. In so many people's homes here, Islām is practiced in a *sharī'ah* manner. So everyone can hear them, they shout, "*Lā ilāha! IllAllāh! Lā ilāha! IllAllāh!*" Then they very slowly drag it out and say, "*Sallallāhu 'alā Muhammad, sallallāhu 'alaihi wa sallam!*"

That is the *sharī'ah*. It is an act, not Sufism. In Islām, that is what is called *sharī'ah*. It is not Sufism. They beat tambourines and shout like fakirs. What they do is an act performed by fakirs. It is not something that can be called Sufism. All of those acts exist within the *sharī'ah*, the first section, a section in which *īmān* is not understood. You must go beyond the act. The act is not Sufism. The meaning is different. They just call those things Sufism.

Sufism is cessation. Sufism is a time of sleeping without sleeping and obtaining well-being. It is a time of speaking without speaking, resting without resting, eating without eating, worshipping without worshipping. There is no outer indication of any of these activities. It is a section in which there are no outward signs.

It is a section unseen on the outside.

Someone could seem to be sitting and speaking, except he would actually be sleeping. He could be sleeping without sleeping. There is no sleep. He speaks without speech. He does not focus on what he sees, he simply looks out. He sees without seeing. He sleeps without sleeping. He eats without eating. He rests without resting. This is how he does things. That is what they say. There is a lot more—it is a great matter.

When we speak of the Qutbiyyah while referring to Muhaiyaddeen ☺, we speak of the ocean of *īmān*.

The ocean of the mind is the ocean of maya. That is why it has been said:

> *The swiftly moving ship sank*
> *in the billowing ocean.*
> *It has been gone for twelve years.*

The billowing ocean is the mind.

> *The swiftly moving ship sank*
> *in the billowing ocean.*
> *It has been gone for twelve years,*
> *gone on the eve of my son's marriage*
> *to the woman he had promised to wed.*

This is how maya, how illusion, is described: The billowing ocean is the mind. It is constantly billowing and rising up, just as waves arise from the ocean. Those were the same waves of illusion that had arisen against the three hundred thirteen *as-hāb*, followers, of Allāh's Rasūl ☺, who had embarked on the ship of truth that is wisdom, who had embraced *īmān* through him.

The old woman's son had set out on the ship of *īmān* twelve years earlier. That swiftly moving ship had sunk to the bottom of the billowing ocean. Her son's *īmān* had sunk to the bottom of the ocean.

By the age of twelve, *īmān* is gone—the *īmān* a person possesses when he is young sinks to the bottom of that ocean, the ocean of maya. The truth sinks.

Determination, certitude, God's speech, and the ability to play and love exist in a child under the age of twelve. He lives in God's heaven then. If he dies before the age of twelve, he gets heaven. The Questioning is less. At the age of twelve he sinks to the bottom of the ocean of maya.

> *The swiftly moving ship sank*
> *in the billowing ocean.*
> *It has been gone for twelve years,*
> *gone on the eve of my son's marriage*
> *to the woman he had promised to wed.*

The old woman's son had drowned in the ocean twelve years before. The twelve years are the twelve openings of the body. The *vangam*, the ship that moves swiftly through that ocean, has sunk in the *angam*, the body, the *qalb*, the heart, the mind. The ship has sunk.

The ship sank and her son died—his *īmān* died. The One God had arranged his marriage. The ship had sunk on the eve of his wedding. It was now twelve years later, the night before the bride promised to him was going to be joined to the *dunyā*, about to marry the darkness of the *dunyā*, the ignorance known as maya.

> *That is why I am weeping in sorrow,*
> *cried the old woman.*

That is how we speak of the Qutbiyyah and *īmān*—the Qutb☺ of *īmān*. The ship has sunk in the *qalb*, sunk in the mind, sunk in maya. It sinks at the age of twelve. It sinks in the twelve openings.

> *That is why I am weeping in sorrow,*
> *cried the old woman.*

That is how the song goes. Yet, it is not like that either.

The Secret of the Shaikh

If we are to learn, we must stay with the Shaikh.

The fragrance abides in the flower. Before that, the fragrance was in the tree. The tree was in the seed, all its qualities were in the seed. After it grows and emerges from the seed, all the leaves and branches that were within it will appear. Everything was within it.

After the fragrance begins to emanate from the flower, how long will the flower remain on the tree? How long will the fragrance last? Possibly three days, or perhaps as long as a week. It will not last any longer than that. The flower will either fall or wither on the branch. The fragrance will depart. As soon as it withers, the smell will be gone.

What should you do if you wish to preserve the flower? If the flower is plucked at the correct time—in the three-day period when it is fully open—if the essence is extracted and the power of the fragrance is distilled, you can preserve the fragrance and the qualities of the flower as an attar, a scent.

The flower has perished. The fragrance has been separated from it, bringing us the knowledge of the kind of flower it came from. Its qualities have been brought to us. Its scent has been brought to us.

The section of the body is like this. It is a thing that will leave after a time. The body is like a flower that lasts only for a certain amount of time. Yet just as we extract the fragrance from the original flower and filter and filter it, if we learn from the Shaikh and filter the essence of what we learn, its fragrance will not die for a very long time. It will last.

If you stay with the Shaikh and join him, taking in the essence of his teachings, there will be no *maut*, no death. The flower has died. The fragrance of the flower has died. Desire has died. Selfishness has died. The *nafs*, the self, has died. They have all died.

If you keep the essence—the original essence, his *insān*

qualities, the fragrance of Allāh, and the essence of his *rūh*, his soul—in a bottle, and touch a drop of it, the fragrance and the qualities will be clearly evident in that drop. You will be able to tell what kind of flower it came from.

That is how you have to be with a Shaikh. You must extract the truth of man before the body perishes.

The recording is turned off and then on again.

TRANSLATOR *Translating what Bawangal ☻ had said while the recording was turned off.* That which belongs to the earth will go back to the earth, but the truth can be extracted and kept.

BAWA MUHAIYADDEEN ☻ —it will come to the other side.

That's all. Very well, now you speak. Speak, speak! Speak about God.

The Secret of My Life
c. 1968

THE QUESTION   Why should we serve the Guru with devotion?[1] And if we do serve him with devotion, what benefit will we attain?

BAWA MUHAIYADDEEN ☺   Our Rare and Most Precious, Great and Almighty Lord, the Lord who permeates everything everywhere, does exist, does He not?

This Lord abides within His devotees as a Slave. He is the Slave within His devotee. He is the Poor One to the poor, the Wealthy One to the wealthy, the Petitioner to the petitioner, the Exalted One to the exalted, the One who can never be evaluated by any criteria. You must contemplate with certitude our Rare and Most Precious, Great and Almighty Lord, the Lord who permeates everything everywhere, the One who is the Devotee to the devotee.

Serving the Guru with devotion means: It is our Rare and Most Precious, Great and Almighty Lord, the Lord who permeates everything everywhere who will clearly be the Devotee within the devotee. It is God Himself who will do that duty.

---

1 to serve, to do duty, with devotion   *Tondu seyya*; a *tondar* is a devotee, a servant, or a slave who serves his Master with utmost love and respect.

Yet we must somehow also come forward to do that kind of duty. Brother, we need to think of every possible meaning of duty and realize within ourselves how we should do that duty. When we come to that realization, we must act accordingly and correct ourselves, knowing that there are some obstacles that need to be scaled if we are to go higher.

If you do not know how to manage those obstacles, the benefits will wither away. If you serve God in the right way, if you elevate your service to God, if you open His umbrella and stand under the shade of that umbrella, no sun, no heat, no fire or flame will ever burn you. They will never harm you.

If you do duty without opening that umbrella, shouting, "Duty! Duty! Duty!" saying you are serving Him without actually serving Him, and substituting something else, you will be dessicated by the sun, soaked by the rain, and undergo so many difficulties, problems, and afflictions.

There are certain conditions that must be met in order to perform devoted service to the Guru. You have to realize them in truth and act accordingly. Listen to every detail. I will tell you later about the benefits I received by doing devoted service to my Guru in my lifetime.

Now to reply to your question: I will tell you how to serve the Guru with devotion and how to benefit from it.

However, brother, the Guru is the Lamp that destroys all three evil qualities, the Flame that dispels the three kinds of darkness. The Guru is the blissful Lamp that drives out and burns away the darkness and evil from the house of the six-pointed star.

If you want to drive out and burn away the darkness from the house of the six-pointed star, the Guru will light the great effulgent Lamp that will dispel the darkness and drive it out.

It is very difficult, brother, to dispel this enormous amount of darkness. Because of the difficulty, you will have to do many duties. That is what is called devoted service to the Guru.

People like me cannot dispel the darkness on the earth. Only those who truly have the capacity to serve God can serve the Guru. When that is done, they can fill the Lamp.

In what kind of state does that duty exist? We have to forget ourselves and do duty to the Guru. You must forget yourself and do the duty to the Guru.

Whom do you have to forget?

THE MAN WHO ASKED THE QUESTION You have to forget the self and do duty.

BAWA MUHAIYADDEEN ☺ Yes, you must forget yourself and do duty to the Guru.

When we say you must forget yourself, it means you have to forget your body, your opinions, and your life itself. The benefit of such service is that you will be able to see the blissful secret of the house of liberation.

Brother, I will tell you. Listen.

You must have certitude of faith in God who is One and believe that His umbrella is resplendently outspread everywhere, sheltering everything. You must accept this truth and its appropriate state. With certitude, you must accept the truth that God exists, that His power is everywhere, that all the worlds are His, all the lands are His. You must have certitude that this truth is the truth.

You must accept the truth that exalted beings and the devotees of the Bestower of Grace have come to abide here in this world in so many forms. We must accept this truth with firm truth. Because God exists, His devotees exist—they have come to the world.

There are nine kinds of precious gems buried in the earth and there are also white stones that you call gems scattered across the surface of the earth that are washed up by the rain. Until you find a real gem, you will exist in a situation in which you will keep insisting, "These are the gems! These are the gems!" about the stones.

Even so, you need to accept the truth about them. There are many varieties of quartz crystals that will look like gems, that will appear with many colors, and lie on the surface of the earth. The real gem could be in the same spot, however, it will be buried somewhere deep below, beneath many layers of earth. It will not be visible to every eye. We have to hunt and search for the real gem with great difficulty until we can find it. We have to undergo so many kinds of hardship to dig out and uncover the real gem.

There are many who deceive people in order to make a living, many who roam the world telling the people that the false gems are the real gem. It is easy to talk about, but difficult to act accordingly. You have to find the real gem.

Here are some words of advice for correcting yourself. I will sing you a song about the way you should act:

> *Tell me,*
> *will the beautiful snake*
> *that lives in the deep jungle*
> *say, "I will freely give you*
> *the gem that is forming in my mouth?"*
> *Look, this itself is an illustration placed before*
> *the disabled people of the world.*
> *It is your solemn duty to be aware*
> *with your own inner awareness that*
> *this is something only a* gnāni *can know.*
>
> *Others will say:*
> *"I am an* ʿālim, *a* mastān, *a* nabī, *a* walī.
> *I am a* gnāni *even more exalted than a Qutb."*
> *This is how they will speak,*
> *those grand* munivars *who fly about*
> *glorifying themselves as* gnānis.

*So many will dress themselves
in so many kinds of disguises
and say so many things like that in the world.*

*They will say:
"Who could possibly be better than me in this birth?"
They will declare:
"Is there anything greater than me in this world?"
They will announce:
"We will replicate everything we see,"
as they teach you about the visions seen by the eyes.
But when the Angel of Death ⊚ comes,
they will be seized by destruction.
But when the Angel of Death ⊚ comes,
they will be seized by destruction
and they will cry out.
Their ordeal is your lot!*

*Perceive the Blissful One through words of wisdom
and reach the Savior of both worlds,
the Savior of both worlds
who dispels the darkness, and fills you with grace,
dispels the darkness, and fills you with grace,
the Blissful One in your home.*

*Lifting the capstone
from the pinnacle of the temple,
he will close his body,
his physical form, and his mouth.
His blissful heart will open and melt.
The flame in the Lamp
made of the fire of the gem
will intensify and burn more brightly.
A true* gnāni *will withdraw, and
be as still as the rain when it stops falling.
He will not indicate where he is
or announce his presence.*

Yet you will see this state
being announced.
All who speak this way will be like
someone who washes a banana leaf in the river
and serves you food on it
after he has eaten and used it as a plate
instead of discarding it.
Although the banana leaf is worth less than a trinket
bought from a roadside stand,
such a person will teach from it as if it were a book
spontaneously emerging from his mouth.

He will discourse about things he has not seen
and everything he says will be worthless.
Observe this and speak to yourself instead.
These great lectures are all worthless,
and those who are taught thus are worthless
and lacking in wisdom.
Such is the chattering wisdom of monkeys without tails,
the chattering wisdom of monkeys without tails.
They will die in the world after suffering
and falling to the ground.
Never accept those lectures or
engrave them in your heart!

There is an essential principle
in which everything is contained:
There are no words more exalted than
"lā ilāha" and "illAllāh."
The words ōm namō nārāyaṇā[2] are the way.

Exhale the "*om*" and inhale the Sīvam—God—and seat Him within. Hold the reins and ride your breath. Exhale the "*om*." Place it outside of yourself. You must draw in God from the outside and seat Him in your heart.

You must sit in front of the Guru, and join with him to

---

2 *ōm namō nārāyaṇā* This is a Sanskrit mantra of those who believe there is only One God.

correct yourself.

"*Lā*" is an Arabic word, a negation. "*Lā ilāha*"—there is nothing other than You. "*IllAllāh*"—You are Allāh.

Exhale from your left nostril, "There is nothing other than You." Inhale from your right nostril, "*illAllāh,*" You are Allāh, the One who gives abundantly without diminishment. Seat this in your heart. Of all mantras, this is the most exalted, the mantra through which you can see the One who exists in the beautiful form of bliss.

You need to have a true Guru for this method of raising and lowering the mantra.

The snake lives in the deep jungle like this. There are such things as cobras, are there not? What is the attribute of the cobra? The cobra has a gem in its mouth. If you go to get it, will you succeed? You will not even be able to catch a glimpse of that cobra!

Will the cobra come to you on its own and tell you, "I have the gem. I will give it to you."? Will the cobra simply spit out the gem and give it to you? It will not give it to you. If you search for it, you will not even catch a glimpse of it.

Where is this beautiful snake? People say that it contains a gem. If you look for it, will you find it? You will not be able to see it. Or do you think the snake will find us and give us the gem for nothing? You cannot find it, nor will it give you the gem for nothing.

Like this, a *gnāni*, a true devotee of God, one who has the truth, will not waste his words of truth. He will give that pearl only to a real pearl. Only if you search and do real duty with real devotion to the real Guru can you receive the benefit.

How can this be done? We have to rid ourselves of the three primal evils—arrogance, karma, and maya. We have to destroy the six[3] hostile forces—lust, hatred, miserliness, lech-

---

3 six   This is expressed here as three times two.

ery, fanaticism, and malicious envy. We have to annihilate the mind that is the enemy to the path. Before duty can be done, we have to endeavor to reject and destroy those evils.

You can serve the good Guru Nādan, a Guru who is a great Master, only after you destroy those evils.

If you yourself cannot destroy them, you will have to destroy them through a Guru Nādan.

This is how it will come into being: If you have a Guru, you will have many kinds of thoughts, use many kinds of abusive language, and take many kinds of forms. You will feel one way if you gain something, wavering between good and bad thoughts, depending upon what you get. None of this is appropriate when serving the Guru with devotion.

If you are in that state, it will not matter whether you do any duty or not. Neither will benefit you. You must destroy these evils and think of your duty to the Guru as a divine duty.

Real service to the Guru can be done only after ridding yourself of the three primal evil qualities, destroying the six hostile forces, and cutting off the enemy to the path that subsequently came to rule you, that caught you when you were five years old.

If you can destroy them and survive, then the blissful secret of service to God and His grace can be obtained.

So, this is the reply to the question you asked. If you wish to try to serve like this, it will not matter whether you serve the Guru or you do not serve the Guru, if all kinds of thoughts come to you.

If you approach the snake and try to snatch the gem out of its mouth, it will bite you. How very subtle you will have to be! You have to be cautious around the snake. You have to persuade the snake to spit the gem into your hand.

It will be a matter of life and death. You have to get the gem without killing yourself—or the snake! So how will you get the gem?

To tame a snake, you have to put out some eggs and many other things, moving them from one place to another, getting the snake to be calm and comfortable until you can place it into a basket. If you do all these things really well, it will spit out the gem.

Then we can live with its light, see its face and much more. If we serve the snake that contains the gem and do these duties until the snake's time comes, it will spit out the gem when it has matured and say, "Brother, take this now. I am leaving."

The Guru's word of grace is the gem. In what state should you act to obtain that gem? You have to be close to the Guru and serve him just as you would serve a snake, giving it what is required, putting those things in its basket. You must make sure you do not get bitten or wounded by its fangs. If you do all these things like an intelligent person, the snake will spit out the gem when it is time for it to leave.

If it spits out the gem and gives it to you, all seven worlds will be brightly illumined. The Light of that gem will be visible in all fourteen worlds.[4]

Any child who serves in this state can see God. It is very difficult, but that is how it has to be done.

However, brother, it will depend upon the kind of service you do in that situation, under those circumstances.

This is the secret of my life. But let's put that secret aside for now.

I will tell you about one of the duties we did for the Guru. We were sixty-three disciples who lived with my Guru Nādan. The sixty-three of us had no differences between us. We had no conflicts between us. We did not look for food or

---

4 fourteen worlds   This is expressed as the two times seven worlds, describing the seven worlds above and the seven worlds below the central world that is the heart of the human being.

clothing, our own welfare, or comforts for our bodies. We loved doing our duty to the Guru and considered it a divine duty. We served him and cared for him. All of us were very concerned about his welfare and his blissful secrets, and the happiness that came from what we were doing with hearts that were his devoted slaves.

However, it depends upon the effort you make and the form you take when you destroy those evil qualities by annihilating the three primal evil qualities, obliterating their forces, and destroying the enemy to the path that subsequently came to rule you.

When you come to such a state, the Guru's gaze will fall upon you. What do you have to do? You have to open the book of your heart for the happiness of the Guru. There must be no mistake or blemish in it. If there is a blemish, the ink will not adhere. And if the ink does not adhere to your book, you will never attain liberation.

But if you stay with the Guru and learn—I will tell you the way to understand with certitude. How do you have to be? You have to dedicate your body, possessions, and soul[5]— all three—to the Guru. You have to surrender your ideas of good and evil to the Guru. You must destroy self-praise. Respect for the Guru must be foremost.

The more you exalt him, the more those exaltations will be recorded in your book. The book is not written, it is stamped. There is no paper and no ink. There is a stamp that comes down with a *tappu, tappu*. Whenever you exalt him or do service to the Guru, the stamp comes down onto the book. The imprint comes down according to the way you do

---

5   body, possessions, and soul   *Udal, porul, āvi*. Because the Guru has no interest in material things, and he will not take even an atom of what belongs to you, *porul* does not refer to your material possessions, but to your possessiveness, your sense of self and what belongs to it, and includes even your most deeply held ideas and opinions.

the duty. What you do, the circumstances, and the way you do it at that particular time will be stamped in the book—*tappu, tappu, tappu, tappu,* sealed there without ink. It is an indelible seal. You cannot erase it. No one in all the universes can erase it. And it is valid in all the universes.

Now, what kind of seal is this, brother? How can you do devoted service to the Guru in order to obtain liberation? If you want to obtain the seal that is not printed with ink, how should you serve him?

There were sixty-three of us children.[6] We listened to his words intently. We did not look up. We looked down, split open our hearts, looked into them, and accepted that path. The Guru's ocean of bliss had to grow. We had to take care of his basic needs and serve him.

How did we do this, brother? It was a duty that had to be done in common for all of creation. How many? We were sixty-three disciples. Sixty-three—?

THE MAN WHO ASKED THE QUESTION Disciples.

BAWA MUHAIYADDEEN ☺ Disciples! We went to look for salvation from the Guru. And what did we sixty-three disciples do? We planted a tree in an open space. But should only the sixty-three of us benefit from that tree? Everyone should benefit from this tree!

Whoever among the sixty-three disciples is a true devotee, for him there is a Lamp inside the seal engraved in his heart. Whatever you feed the Guru, whatever food you give the Guru will be recorded there.

If you give him milk, the benefit for having done so will be sealed in your book. If you give him poison, then poison will be sealed in your book. The result of whatever you give

---

6   children   This does not refer to age or kinship, but the closeness of the bond with the Guru.

him, whether it is sugarcane or treacle or anything else, will be printed in your book.

You can do service and you can give things to the Guru whether you are seen or unseen by others, whether you are with him or not.

The Guru will keep his mouth wide open—*Ah!*—no matter what you feed him and without knowing what you pour into him. If you pour in poison, the Guru will not know it. If you pour in raw fruit, the Guru will not know it. If you pour in milk, the Guru will not know.

The seal comes from another place. It comes from there, to be stamped here. There will be a stamp for each thing you do. The seal will be fixed depending upon the result that will come from what you feed him. It cannot be known. The seal depends upon the state and the beauty with which you act, and this is what you will completely, absolutely, surely, and exactly experience.

Do not think: *How long is this going to take? Are we going to be here forever? We are just ordinary people who live in the world.*

You will actually be in the world for only one week, yet still, you may have to stay at the same level for many, many thousands of weeks. There are many levels, and you may get caught. It is only a week. Do not think, *What is going on? What is this swami,* this *sannyāsi, doing*? You may have to live with this *sannyāsi* for thousands and thousands of eons. The seal will be stamped during that time. Although it is stamped here, do not look for it here.

That Treasure, the Treasure which is held in common by all—how should you love it and hold on to it?

Let us imagine that there is a Teacher somewhere who belongs equally to everyone. You must have certitude and determination. Everyone who comes to that tree must pour water onto it. The tree needs water in order to grow. The sixty-three people have to water it. The tree must grow tall. You planted it as a tiny seedling, and now others have to water it, and then still others have to water it, and then still others have to water it. It will grow tall. As it grows, the branches will emerge. And as the branches emerge, they will spread out in all four directions, and develop flowers and leaves.

Then more shade will come. When the shade comes, cows, goats, chickens, cranes, and little birds will arrive to rest under it. An occasional human being too will come, saying, "This is good shade. Let's lie down and rest here for a while before we proceed. What a blessed person must have planted this tree in the intolerable sun!" They will praise the person who planted it, and rest under it.

Cows and goats will come to lie down under it. They might defecate, they might urinate, and all of it will just be fertilizer for that tree: the tree will take it in and grow even taller. It will draw in the fertilizer and grow tall. As it grows, even more branches will develop, and they will spread out even further.

As it grows and grows, thousands and thousands of animals, cows, goats, human beings, and other beings will come to sit under it. Birds will come to sit on branch after branch. They will stay there night and day. As time goes by, parrots, mynas, and all kinds of birds will come. They will stay for the night. You too can stay there day and night and find comfort and happiness.

Many kinds of fruit will grow on the tree. As the tree grows bigger, more and more fruits will emerge. As the fruits grow, you can pick and pick and eat them.

You can eat, and if you keep watering and fertilizing the tree, those who come to the tree can also help to water and fertilize the tree and keep the area around the tree clean. They can also pick and eat the fruits. This person can pick and eat the fruits, that person can pick and eat the fruits, this person can pick and eat the fruits, that person can pick and eat the fruits. The reward will be commensurate with the devoted duty that is done. You will receive the fruit that is meant for you there.

That is the seal, the seal, the seal! It will be stamped, *tappu, tappu, tappu*! The work done there is all stamped and sealed.

The tree grows and grows, taller and taller, up into the heavens. The higher it grows, the more the sixty-three children and the city will benefit. The city will prosper. The storms, the thunder, and the lightning all will be blocked by the tree.

The tree that stands in the open space can withstand so many kinds of storms and hurricanes and fiery currents of air. Even if a typhoon comes to try to destroy the city, the tree will confront it and safeguard the city. It will stop the typhoon and turn it into a gentle breeze. The tree will block the hurricane. All the lightning and the thunder will be absorbed by the tree.

As the tree grows, you will not be harmed by any of these storms. Harm and sorrow will not approach you. You can cheerfully rest under the tree in any kind of weather and not a drop of rain or sun will fall upon you.

So the harder you work to make the tree grow, the taller it will become. As you keep watering, watering, and feeding the tree, it will draw in all the nourishment and grow high into the heavens. As the branches grow and spread out, so many birds will come, so many parrots will come, so many doves will come, every day.

The birds in the world and the birds in the heavens will come. All the people in the world will come to rest. The more they hear and hear and hear the sound of those birds, the more happiness there will be. They can dwell in the shade. The city will prosper.

As the tree grows, you will grow, and the name of the

person who planted the tree will grow. It will flourish. They will bless the person who planted it, saying, "He is a blessed person." They will say, "Our illnesses will be healed and we can rest there when we are tired."

The sixty-three of us watered the tree. If you keep on watering the Guru like that, and if you sweep and clean under that tree, your names too will grow.

More birds will come, more birds will come, more birds will come, more birds will come—every kind of bird will be under the tree—birds you have not seen, birds you cannot imagine. You will see scenes you have never seen before. You will see wonders you have never seen before. The tree will continue to grow, and all who shelter under it will need food.

But never think, *Why are they eating? Why are these parrots eating here?*

As the tree grows and grows, it will develop into an imperishable tree. It will be immensely tall.

Never think, *I planted it. Why are you eating from it?* There are many stories about it.

You have planted Mutavalli's tree. Your name will grow as the tree grows. The city will grow. The region will grow. The tree will block any evil that might otherwise approach. It will destroy so many kinds of distress. It will put out fires. It will destroy bombs and explosive devices.

The city will be elevated, the people will be elevated, the entire region will thrive and be absorbed in the good path. Everything will be elevated in this state.

This tree is called the Guru.

How should you treat this Guru—the true Guru? The seal will be stamped depending on how you do this. It will be obvious.

You must not try to cut down that tree.

Never think, *There is another man eating from the tree I planted! I watered it, and now these parrots are eating all the fruit.* No! Let the share that is meant for the parrot go to the parrot. Ten times more goes to the man who watered the tree. The raw fruits are up above, the ripe fruits on the low branches will all be yours. When they hear the sound of a person, the birds will fly up to those raw fruits. Those fruits are for them. The fruits lower down are for you. You can eat them when they are perfectly ripe.

Do not think you should eat the fruit when it is unripe. Right now you are thinking of eating the fruit when it is raw. Do not eat raw fruit. Wait until the fruit ripens. No one is going to pick the fruit that is meant for you.

You have the elixir that will make the fruits ripen. If you water the tree and take care of it in the right way, the ripe fruits will come to you. Then you will get seventy thousand different tastes from them.

There is much more to this story.

When I say certain things in an open way, you sometimes may think I am talking about you. Those things are within you. Whatever I say, whatever issue I speak of, whether it is about the subtlety of wisdom or duty to God, I say, "Correct yourself and come to the good path."

Whenever I tell you about God, you think, Aday, *this is my story. This is for me. That is for you.* You separate what I say and you think, *This is for me.*

You do that because of your own bad thoughts.

The *swāmiyār* does not think like that when he speaks. He tells these things to you for your own benefit. If the child is to benefit, the child must embrace what he says and accept it.

The good Guru Nādan is here to destroy your horrible qualities. There is an old adage, "The good Guru Nādan does not kill, he does not kill." He is only telling you these things to drive out your horrible qualities, not to kill you.

Each one of you gets up to leave when you think, *He's talking to me. Appā, that's about me! What is this? He's talking to me!* No, I speak only to correct you. Try to eat.

Do you try to eat the fruit and correct yourself? No. I speak so that you can correct yourself, partake of the fruit, and come to my Father. It is not just for you, it is for all the children.

If only you could realize your own faults, mistakes, and missteps for each section and level, and remember, Aday. *What I did was wrong*, and then take in what comes next!

Look intently, listen intently.

You must think, *When I drank water over there, the Guru told me there was a worm in it. Ah ha! That was wrong, so I must not do it again. When I went to eat, I was critical of a certain person. It happened like that under those circumstances. Oh, I must not say things like that from now on.*

Correct yourself.

A child who takes in each section and stops doing those things is a good child, the Guru's son, the Guru's child.

Mostly, I just bray like a donkey at you. The way in which you act, *appā*, shows that you do not listen to what I say. You will get the corresponding result—the seal will fall. What can I do about that by shouting at you? Which gem goes to whom means that a gem must know the gem.

He who corrects himself will get it.

Yet you speak in many ways, saying, Ha! *This is for me! That is for you! It is that way! It is this way! It is that way!* while you rudely leave here without saying a word. When I look at you and tell you about this situation and the subtle details in it, I feel like laughing.

However, when we have been given a restriction—no matter where we were when we made the mistake—as soon as we come to the Guru, we have to understand from the Guru's words, *Oh! What I did was wrong.* Aday, appā, *I must not do it again.*

You must immediately look for your next mistake. *I drank*

water here. That was wrong. Aday, the Guru was speaking of that and I did that. I must not do it again.

We have to correct ourselves. Yet you do not correct yourself like that. You keep saying, "This is mine. That is yours."

I do not know what to say about what you have in your hearts. If you act like this when you serve the Guru, you will not get the stamp. Do you understand that you will not get it?

THE MAN WHO ASKED THE QUESTION Yes, Swami.

BAWA MUHAIYADDEEN ☺ If you are going to serve the Guru outside of the restrictions, there will be no benefit if you do and no benefit if you do not. Both are the same. If you serve him it is the same as not serving him.

If you can serve him with the heart that I have described and grow the tree, saying, "Let everyone eat. Let me eat the fruits I came to eat while the others eat the other fruits," this is the restriction you have to observe when you do this duty.

I am speaking like this believing that you will correct your thoughts. Correct them at least from now on! *Ha?*

This is mine, that is yours must never exist in your heart. You must not do this from now on. This issue is wrong! You must correct yourself.

But even listening to words like these is disgusting to you. You are ashamed when you hear the words I speak.

As you get up and run away, you think, Aday. Ha? *What I did has come out here into the open!*

You do not think, *I simply should not do it again in the future.*

Instead of thinking, Aday, *I stood and urinated there,* you say, *He's talking about me,* and you run away.

No. You should think, *From now on, I must not stand there and urinate. I must go to the correct place, a place concealed from others, and then relieve myself carefully.*

The Secret of My Life

You still have not corrected yourself. When I look at your thoughts, your training, your standards, and your form, I do not know what kind of seal you will get. What seal will you get? The seal comes down according to what you do.

Now look—I am here saying these words. However, the seal comes from there. You are trying to see how the Guru is doing it. You think it is done by man. It is done by God. See how subtly the seal comes down.

You think, *The restriction is here, so I can do it over there.*

It is not like that. You think it is all happening here.

It is a seal stamped by the Rare, Most Precious, All-Pervasive Lord. He makes it happen. Do not think the seal will be stamped in the way you want it to be. These are the true words of that Wise and Able One, the Rare, Most Precious, All-Pervasive Lord. You must believe them with certitude.

If you correct your mistakes one by one, it is certain that you will be able to serve the Guru with devotion and receive the rightful benefit. You will receive the benefit for the words you hear. Brother, these are the ways to do devoted service to the Guru.

You can reach the refuge at the feet of God when you destroy the millions and millions of things you have to correct and destroy in yourself.

So, where is it? It is not in a temple, a stone, or a brass idol, nor does it exist here or there. God's Temple of Divine Duty is formed by God. God's Temple exists in the corrected human being. God will dwell in a corrected human being who has destroyed the three primal evil qualities, the six hostile forces, and the enemy to the path that subsequently came to rule him.

It is through such a human being that you can obtain the rewards for your austerities—not in a temple, not here, not there. It cannot be described. You can get this only through such a human being. God exists in the Temple of Divine Duty.

This Rare, Great, Most Precious, Formless God is there. He will talk to you from there with this tongue.

THE MAN WHO ASKED THE QUESTION This happens in the heart of the devoted servant, Swami, where God dwells.

BAWA MUHAIYADDEEN ☉ *Ah!* That is His abode. That is the Temple. That is the Divine Temple. That is the Temple of Divine Duty. That is the Temple of Liberation. That is the Temple of the Three-eyed One. It cannot be described, *appā*. It is there that the fourteen worlds exist. God is the Devoted Servant within the devoted servant. He is the Poor Man to the poor man. He is the High-ranking to the high-ranking and the Low-ranking to the low-ranking. He is the Able One. Where does He abide? The Guru lights the Lamp within the devoted servant. If you serve the Guru in the right way, all the gems and pearls that need to be given to you will be given—depending upon how you do your duty.

However, if you are thinking of cutting down the tree you planted, you need to realize that the tree has grown up through the sky. You say, "I planted it, it cannot live without me," and you try to cut it down.

The tree is rooted in the east where the sun rises, and it has grown. It has grown right up to the heavens—all the branches, flowers, and fruits are there where the sun sets in the west—there the benefit is greater.

If you try to cut down the tree, you will not be able to hack out as much as a splinter. You would be able to cut only in the small area where you exist. The tree extends throughout all the villages, towns, and cities. The branches and the fruits and the flowers are all elsewhere.

As the tree grows higher and higher into the heavens, you can stay there under it in a good way for all time. You can abide there with so much wealth. You can keep on eating the everlasting fruits. You can obtain the undiminishing wealth.

Only in that realm can the wonder of the tree be understood. When the tree is there, all lives will come to abide under it. They will say, "*Aday, appā,* there is a tree like that on this island." *Ha, ha, ha, ha,* they will praise it, and they also will praise the elders who are caring for the tree. Those are the disciple-children. The true disciple-children.

You have to carefully and tenderly search for this state. It is done in many ways. You must do each thing with effort. There is much to be gained. Look deep within yourself. Succeed on the good path. Come in a good way. While it is like that...*eh,* shall we let all these things be for now? Brother, what else did you want to ask?

THE MAN WHO ASKED THE QUESTION   Swami, how can we know the true Guru, the true *gnāni*?

BAWA MUHAIYADDEEN☉   I told you about the devoted service you need to do. The knowledge will unfold when the benefit of the duty comes to be known by you.

You must destroy the three primal qualities, the six hostile forces, and the enemy to the path that subsequently came to rule you.

When you destroy them, dispose of them, and look, you will see the true Guru. In this state, you will understand the ideals of the true Guru I have been describing.

The meanings are within what I have been describing. Thus, if you are to do devoted service like this, you must look at the state being described.

In my life, this was how we asked our Guru Nādan questions.

How can we ask him now? We do not ask those questions now, although when we think of them, he will give us the answers. If we think of the questions, he will tell us. Those were the blessings he gave us.

Have we finished talking about the Guru issue, *appā*? Ask what else you need to ask. Ask the next question.

THE MAN WHO ASKED THE QUESTION Yes, Swami. When we do service to the Guru, what benefit can we attain from the Guru?

BAWA MUHAIYADDEEN ☺ You can attain either heaven or hell, can you not? There are millions of words to describe the benefit. I only gave you one example: how the tree has to grow and how the duty has to be done. You can attain either heaven or hell. You can attain either good or evil. And that is just one meaning, is it not?

The Secret Book
December 6, 1973

Anbu. My love. *Vanakkam*, greetings, to the children, the loving children who are the jeweled lights of my eyes. There is an explanation you need to understand. It is only if we conclusively know and understand this explanation that we will be able to understand the truth that exists within it.

There are differences between the experiences you have with the Guru—what you learn from the Guru—and what you read in books. The difference between the sections you learn from books and the sections you learn from the Guru is that the lessons you learn from the Guru are alive. There is a power that comes from those lessons that promotes understanding. The lessons have *hayāh*. They are alive. A clear understanding comes from them. The Guru's help is there. He can speak to you from there. He can make you understand from there.

There are many, many such differences. What is learned from books has no *hayāh*, it is dead. It will not speak to you. It will not make you understand. It will not ward off danger. It is a lesson that exists in silence—it will not speak. Even if you learn it, it will not talk to you. Even if you take a picture of it, it will not bring you any explanation. It exists in silence, it is mute.

What you learn from a Guru can bring you understanding. Yet, children, loving children, jeweled lights of my eyes, there is an explanation. When we study with a Guru, we need to record in our hearts all the points of each explanation he gives in the same way that we record his explanations on tape. You must endeavor to record every point in your heart without missing anything. Whether he is giving an explanation of hell or heaven or man or anything else, you must endeavor to use the right microphone, turn on the right switch, and check in the right way to make sure it is all being recorded correctly. You must check to make sure that everything you hear every minute, every moment of every day, is recorded.

That treasury book will be the uncompromised account book in which all the details of your life-business are written. It is a secret book. Even though you may have other books for income tax, business, and so forth, the accounts in your treasury book—all the profits and the losses—are in that secret book.

A company may have such a book. Even if there are a hundred shareholders in that company, the primary manager will have a secret book written by the accountant and his clerk. That book will be a deep secret between the chief clerk, the accountant, and the manager. That book will contain the receipts for the many complications in the business, the most secret matters, of things that could have been deleted, or corrected, or increased, or decreased—decreased for income tax or hidden from the government.

Similarly, no matter how many books you may have read or how many businesses you may own, you need to pick up the book of your secret life. That secret needs to be there. That book needs to contain the sections regarding your birth, the histories of your ancestors, the explanations of

The Secret Book

the states in which you previously existed, the explanations of your schooling, the explanations of the husband-wife relationship in your life, the explanations of your livelihood, the explanations of the hunger and illness in your life, the explanations of your kingdom, the explanations of all the decisions you have made, and the explanations of whether you will go to hell or heaven.

You must record those explanations so your Guru can teach you the lessons that need to be extracted from those explanations. Then he will give you the record of your life since the time you were born. You must take it all into your secret book, into that tape. You must preserve those histories and record them.

You must carefully adjust the switches, position the microphone, and record the explanations without missing anything. Before you can begin to record, you must conscientiously check the battery levels, the electric circuits, whether the microphone is working, and whether the sounds are being correctly reproduced.

If you do not check those things, the section coming for that time will slip away without being written in the book. It will not be recorded. Then that day's history and your analysis will be missing—they will not appear in the book.

Thus, these are the sections you must take in from the Guru every day and put into the uncompromised account book that is the book of your life. They must be recorded. You must record them every day and then get the book printed. As that book is being dictated about all your histories, about the world, about maya, about hell, about the *dunyā*, the world, and about desire, each one must be imprinted in your Perception, Awareness, Intellect, Assessment, Wisdom, Discerning Wisdom, and Divine Luminous Wisdom.

If you can individually record each event into your Awareness, you will be able to read the book later.

When you read it, there will be a vibration that will be able to speak. When you read it and remember, taking each event into your Awareness, turning that Awareness into Perception, taking that into your Intellect and Assessment, the explanation will come from it as it arrives in each level of Awareness. When you think of the book and remember, the vibration—the speech—will come from it. When you read the book, you will be able to see the meaning of every record, every breath, every word—you will be able to speak and speak with it. Then the explanations of the histories will be made known to you. The original events will be made comprehensible to you.

Unless you do the recording correctly, the book will not speak to you. You will not be able to examine your story.

If you do the recording correctly, you will be able to know the history of the microcosm and the macrocosm. However, the record must be here. You must speak with it. Your Awareness must read it and reveal it to you. Your Perception must understand what it is. Your Intellect must explain what kind of thing it is. Your Assessment must reveal the original agreement and show you an estimate of your expenses to date, the profit, and the loss.

Assessment will show us an estimate of the profits and losses incurred in our life between the time we came from there to live here until we leave from here to go there. It will give us all the explanations of the estimates in our life. It will provide us with that map.

The wisdom of the senses, the wisdom of the five elements, will point out the details. *Oh! This happened when I went this way; that happened when I went that way. That was where I made the mistake.*

If you have done the recording, Discerning Wisdom will make it right and erase the wrong when you read the book. It will all be communicated to you during that conversation.

The Secret Book

As you remember and remember and ask the Guru, you will realize, *Ah! That was that way, this was this way, this was this way.* You must show it to the Guru. You must show your Awareness everything the Guru has said. Then you can speak to him. If that Awareness is within you when you speak to the Guru having retained what he has said, and if you too are there, you will be able to understand. You can look at all the explanations. You can speak with everything. You can understand all the powers. Then you can speak.

Intellect must hold up the book, reveal how you spoke, and what the issue was. As soon as it reveals that to you and your Wisdom sees it, the Guru will tell you what it was actually like. "Look at this television! Look at this radio! Look how the sound is coming from it! This sound is coming from this station. That sound is coming from a wireless station."

He will tell you which sound is coming from which station. "This sound is coming from God. This sound is coming from maya. This telephone call is coming from hell. This telephone call is coming from satan. This telephone call is coming from the senses. This is coming from desire. This is coming from a hypnotic delusion. This is coming from ignorance. This is coming from true wisdom. This is coming from Allāh's Nūr. Did you look at this television? Did you hear the sounds of this radio?"

As you remember each one, it will speak. The Guru will teach you. If you stay with him in the right way and see like this, you will see the Guru in front of you. If you take ganja and opium, you will not understand—you will understand only what you have.

If—after having placed the Guru there in the right way, having retained what he has said, having preserved what he has spoken of—you look straight ahead, you will see him in front of you. If you look within, you will see him there. The sound will come. The form will be visible. The speech will come. The manifestation will come by itself. The sound will come by itself to give the explanation. Like this, like this, you will see wonder after wonder. What do you want to see? Do you want to see hell? He has told you about hell.

You have to show him hell—the explanations he has given about hell. You need to say, "My Father, what is hell like? You said there were seven hells."

Whether you open your eyes or close your eyes, you will see. Just think of something and remember it. Then think of your Father and what he has told you. When you remember him, the moment you think of that story and him, he will say, "*Ah!* This is hell," showing it to you.

It is as if you were being shown something in a mirror placed in front of you. You must remember! You must take out the history and show it to him. If you have preserved what he has said, you must take out the book. If you have it and then you speak to him, asking from within that Awareness, that Intellect, that Wisdom, "Father, what is this like?" you will see it directly in front of you. If you look here, you will see it here. If you look straight ahead, you will see it in front of you.

He may say, "Don't look here. Look over there! Look over there—close your eyes and look over there!" You will see it there. The sound will come, the speech will come, the talking will come, the meaning will come, and its explanation will come. It will be like watching a television. The sound will come. The sound will come from the other side, from the telephone. The sight will come from the other side. The sound will come from the other side. The speech will come from the other side. Then you will be able to see it face-to-face. It speaks! It understands.

If you do not take out the book and show it to him, he will not do this. If your Guru is not with you, he will not do this. If you are not there, it cannot speak. This is how you

The Secret Book

must understand. This is how your memory must record every word. You must put every event into your book, into your uncompromised account book. You must put it all into the book of your life.

If you do, he will explain the fourteen worlds to you. If you have recorded everything he says, he will explain your life, the life of God's creation, and give you the explanations of the sun and the moon; the explanations of the hells and the heavens; the explanations of creation; the explanations of the oceans and the hills; the explanations of the air, the earth, and the fire; the explanations of the water—creation; the explanations of the ether; the explanations of the land; the explanations of the lives; the explanations of God; the explanations of the *malā'ikah*, the angels; the explanations of the *ambiyā'*, the prophets; the explanations of the lights; the explanations of wisdom; the explanations of *agnānam*, ignorance; the explanations of *poygnānam*, false wisdom; the explanations of *vingnānam*, scientific wisdom; the explanations of *gnānam*, divine wisdom; the explanations of man; the explanations of the animals; the explanations of caste; the explanations of the religions; and the explanations of "I" and "you." He will explain everything. He will explain every story.

If you do not record the Guru's words, if you do not take them out and show them to him...You have to take them out and look at them! You must remember the Guru, take out the book, and ask for the explanation! This is how it is. Then the sound will come. The speech will come. And you will see the Guru. You will see the explanation of what is in the book. You will see the right and the wrong of it. You will see that this is the meaning of what you asked.

Otherwise, you may have to go there. You may need to see the actual place. If you ask, "What is it that is heaven?" if you remember a little like that, concentrate intensely like that, and look at the Guru, he could say, "Come, let's go." You will go to heaven while you are there.

You and the Guru will speak, and heaven will approach you. When it comes to you, you will see heaven. "This is heaven," the Guru will say. "These are the steps. This is the explanation." Heaven will immediately approach you, and you will look at it.

"*Ah*! I have seen it," you will say.

"What else do you want to see?" the Guru will ask.

"I want to see God. What is God like?" you will say.

You will get the answer in the blink of an eye, the moment you say this.

The sound will come: "God has no form. Within what do you intend to see Him? What shape will you question? How will you see God? What is He like? Who are you? Who is God? Who am I? Who is your Guru? Who are you?"

Here you will see three resplendences. They have no form. The Light will be so bright that you will be unable to look at it. God is there. The Guru is here. You are there. These are the three lights you will see. You must retain every memory, every point of wisdom with certainty. You must hold on and preserve them. Then if you ask your questions with Perception, Awareness, and Wisdom, the explanation will come. Then you can see the microcosm and the macrocosm. You can see the world of hell. You can see the eight heavens. You can see every precious gem there, atom by atom. You can see the *malā'ikah*, the jinns, the fairies, and the 124,000 *ambiyā'* there.

However, you need the names and the words the Guru spoke. Only if you have the names and the words can you show him the Awareness, the words, and the actions. Only if you show them to him like that will the explanation come.

Do not search for God there. Do not search for God here. God is within you. If your Shaikh gives you the wisdom to see God, if your Sayyid gives it to you—and if he is a true

Sayyid, if he is a true Shaikh, if he is a true Qutb, if he is a true Light, if he is truly teaching you—you can see the explanation wherever you are. You can see everything, no matter where you are.

You can see all the explanations in your *qalb*, your innermost heart. You can see the eighteen thousand universes. You can see all the creations God has created. There are seventy thousand moons—you can see them. There are seventy thousand suns—you can see them. You can see so many millions of stars. You can see the explanations and the reverberations within them. You can see the seventy-three groups of humankind. You can see the explanations in every heart. When you look intently, you can see the vibrations in those hearts.

When you look intently like that, you can see the inner form of each person. Outwardly he has a human face. When you look into him, you will see his *sūrah*, his form. If he is a *hayawān*, a beast, you will see a *hayawān*. If he is a snake, you will see a snake.

If you have taken in and preserved the Guru's words, if you have recorded those words, if you have placed him within yourself, you will see that form as soon as you think of doing so. You will know what that person is. Is he a beast? A snake? You will understand what he is, and then you can escape from him. You can understand him, you can know him. Is he a *shaitān*? Is he a demon? You can understand.

If you keep asking about each situation, each explanation, you will see. If you listen to something here but abandon it further on, this is not the *shart*, the correct way. If you listen to this and then simply move on, that is not the *shart*. Therefore, the record must be correct. If you have that record book here inside, the explanation must come to you through it. It is talking—it is a thing that speaks.

If you keep the words of the Guru with you, you can

see all the things that cannot be seen. You can know all the things that cannot be known. You can describe all the things that cannot be described. All the jinns and fairies will burn to a crisp the moment you stare intently at them. *Shaitān* will not come near you. Maya will not come near you. Nothing can bite you without permission. They can only approach you after they have asked for permission.

Therefore, you have to preserve the Guru's words accurately. This is not something you can see in a hypnotic delusion. This is the meaning that can be seen within wisdom as Wisdom. This is the meaning that can be seen within the Guru as the Guru. This is the meaning that can be seen within perception as Perception. This is the meaning that can be seen within certitude as Certitude. This is the meaning that can be seen within God as God. This is the meaning that can be seen within man as Man. This is how the meaning is seen!

However, there is a difference between this kind of wisdom and book-knowledge-wisdom. Book-knowledge-wisdom is a silent study. This is truth, a living lesson. This is the study of our life. Thus, you must do the recording correctly. And you must be prepared to explain it.

You can pray [to see God]. What is prayer? Who can pray to God? How is it done? Is it done by going to a mosque? If you go, will God come to you? If you go to the mosque, will He come to you? If you go to church, will He come to you? Can you see God like that? If you go to the temple, can you see Him? If you bore a hole into a small idol and wear it as a pendant around your neck, can you see God? If you wear little idols, can you see God? Can you see God? You cannot. If we wear a cross, can we see God? Some people wear the Qur'ān as a pendant around their neck. Can God be seen like that? Some people tie a Bible around their waist. Can God be seen like that? Some people tie up the *panjacharam*, the five letters, and wear them. Can God be seen like that?

That is no good! God can never be seen like that. He cannot be seen by doing those things.

In Hinduism, they do a three-times *pūjā* to see God. They bow to a deity, an idol, three times. We go to the church or the mosque three, four, or five times a day. Can God be seen like that? How many minutes are there in a day? [1,440] How many minutes do we spend at the temple? There are twenty-four hours in a day. How many hours go to waste? How many hours will a man spend for the sake of God? How many minutes will he dedicate to God? Perhaps ten minutes at a time. Yet does he actually remember God for even a minute? He looks around there, there, there, here and everywhere during those ten minutes.

In Islām, a man will pray the five-times prayer. How many minutes does he concern himself with God? Five minutes for *subh*, the pre-dawn prayer. Five minutes for *zuhr*, the noon prayer. Five minutes for *'asr*, the afternoon prayer. Five minutes for *maghrib*, the post-sunset prayer. Five minutes for *'ishā'*, the night prayer. Twenty-five minutes!

Can we say he has actually spent twenty-five minutes for God? He has disposed of these twenty-five minutes of the day. How many hours are there in a day? Twenty-four! He works for eight hours and sleeps for eight hours—he expends sixteen hours for work and sleep. He bathes and relaxes for three hours. He eats for three hours. Three plus three is six. That is twenty-two hours. This is how the time goes by as he uses those twenty-four hours.

He may have squandered those twenty-five minutes here in the mosque—we do not know if he has spent even one of those minutes thinking of God. How many hours are there in a year? [8,760 hours; 525,600 minutes] How many hours has he wasted? How many hours has he spent for God?

Look at this. Think of this. At most, a person may have spent about 2,500 minutes for God. The rest of the time he squanders his life. Did he worship the One who gave him food? No. You cannot see God like this. This is not worship. Is this how to pray to the One who has taken care to give you food and water, the One who gives you love and refuge, the One who judges you? No.

What do we do with each intention? What did I do when I went to the mosque? I folded my arms after the *takbīr*, I focused on Him, I remembered Him, I bowed to Him and did the *sajdah*, the prostration, to Him. This is what I did. This is what we do when we go to the mosque. We remember Him as we kneel. This is how we remember Him. This is the five minutes. Isn't that five minutes wasted? Is this how to worship God? No!

We must worship Him day and night, as we inhale and exhale each breath. There are 43,242 breaths in a twenty-four hour day. To remember Him with those breaths; to place our intention upon Him with every breath; to place our intention upon Him with every word; to remember Him every minute; to perceive Him every minute with our Perception; to bring Him into our Awareness every minute; to think of Him every minute within our Intellect; to analyze every minute with Assessment; to understand every minute with Wisdom; to use Discerning Wisdom every minute to discern and reveal the truth of the difference between the world, God, and man; to have faith; to intensely remember every minute that there is nothing other than God—this remembrance is prayer. This intention is prayer. This thought is prayer. This kind of worship is prayer. What you remember there in this state is prayer. That is what this is.

Endeavor to think of it. This is what is called prayer. You cannot spend twenty-five minutes and expect to reach heaven.

And what do you do as a congregation there in the mosque for those twenty-five minutes? *O God! My business is failing! My business is running at a loss. Make my business do well, O God! My wife is sick. Heal her, O God! I have no child, give me a boy, O God! I have no job, give me a job, O God! That man has denounced me, destroy him, O God! Kill him. He has set up a business next to mine, and he is competing with me. Eradicate him.*

What does he do? What do we do? This is what we do. This is not prayer, but this is how our prayers go. This is how our five minutes go by: *O God, give me heaven! O God, there is an extremely beautiful woman, give me a way to make her my wife! I have a desire like that young man has, give me what I want! Does God have no eyes? Does my Guru have no pity? Is he testing me? Is that why I am sick?*

This is how we pray. This is how we do everything. *O God, I have no money. I have to travel. Help me!* This is what you do. Is this worship? What are you worshipping for the sake of God? This is how you spent those twenty-five minutes. This is not the way.

God is worshipped every minute, every moment with every thought. To remember Him in your Awareness; to remember Him in your intention; to see Him in your gaze; to draw Him in through your Wisdom; to manifest Him in your heart—when all your thoughts and your entire life remember Him, that is worship. That is prayer. That is the intention. That is the focus. That is the true worship we perform.

It is through doing this that we need to understand our life and the *qudrah*, the power, of God. We need to know this explanation. Worship is to remember God and to see Him without allowing Perception, Awareness, Intellect, Assessment, Wisdom, Discerning Wisdom, or Divine Luminous Wisdom to fluctuate. This is the work a human being will do.

Then he will understand right and wrong. He will understand man and satan. He will understand man and beast. He will understand God and maya. He will understand darkness and Light. He will understand ignorance and true wisdom. He will understand truth and falsehood. He will understand anger and forgiveness. He will understand morality and immorality. He will understand good and evil. He will understand what the "I" and the "you" are. He will understand right and wrong. He will understand hell and heaven. He will understand who God is and who satan is. He will understand which food is good and which food is bad. He will understand the essence from which evil is created, and the essence from which what is right is created.

To study the wisdom that can understand in this way, you must endeavor to learn wisdom from the Guru. To worship God, you must search with this Awareness. To remember Him with every movement is worship. To look at Him with every gaze and to forsake evil is worship. When every thought stands within Him, sees from there, and thinks from there, that is worship.

You must remember each thing that happened when you were with your Shaikh and what he said. Then, through the Guru, you must understand it all by means of each point in your secret book. This remembrance is called worship.

If you do not take it in, if you whine, "But I have not seen God!" I would have to reply, "Didn't you make the recording?"

If you say, "But I have not seen the Light!" I would have to reply, "Don't you have the history?"

If you say, "Where is it?" I would have to reply, "Don't you have it? Didn't you record it? Didn't you look at it with Awareness and preserve it? Didn't you read it? You just read book knowledge. You only preserved silence. You did not keep the life. How can you see it? The silence does not speak. Give up the books. The Guru has given you a living thing. It is a vibration. It is a magnet. It has *hayāh*, life. If you had kept that living thing, it would not just be there, it would move.

Then you would understand. Then you would understand where that living thing has journeyed before. Then you would know all the places it has been. Then when it awakens you afterward, you would see it.

"But you possess a thing that does not move, a silent thing. That is not the way. You must truly understand. You must truly know. That is a moving thing, a magnetic thing, a living thing, a bright thing, a true explanation, a Light that brings the explanation. It is an everlasting treasure. If you had kept that treasure, it would continuously have given you the explanation. It would have read the story the moment you picked it up. As soon as you turned the page and remembered the history, it would have come to you. That is how it is."

Children, look a little. This is how you must do it. Capture and keep the history precisely. Do the recording perfectly for the uncompromised account book. May the secret book, the life book, be correct. If you record it accurately, listen to the explanations correctly, and keep it precisely, that will be the uncompromised account book for the Guru, for God, and for you. Just as only the manager, the chief clerk, and the accountant know the real numbers, that secret will be known only to the Guru, to you, and to God. Then you can understand the math. Then you can know the explanation.

That is the Muchudar, the Triple Flame. Three Lights. Three Resplendences.

Therefore, give up all these other things. If you keep the silent things here and there, and if you play with them as you yank at a silent puppet, it is not the Guru's fault. This is what you need to understand. Take it in and try to check it in this way. Take it in and try to thoroughly examine it. Do not just take it in and thoroughly examine it like this, but also try to very profoundly reflect upon it. Do not just profoundly reflect upon it, but try to explore it. Do not just explore it, but intermingle with it and look at the explanation. Not only that, but test it. Then you will understand. Do not just test it, but understand the reward that comes from it. Then you will know. Find out what the profits and losses are. Then you will know. Find out: will it perish, will it change, or will it be unchanging? You need to do more research. It will never change on its own. It will only change when you change. It will not change if you do not change. It is everlasting.

This, children, is what you must think about. What you are learning is fine, your coming here is fine, your being here is fine, your seeing the Guru is fine, your being here to listen is fine—but you have to do it this way. Only if you do it this way can you get the reward. If you act in the way we have described, you can obtain its benefit. You can obtain its explanation. You can reach its resonance. You can know the power that understands you and God.

Each child must gain this benefit. It is essential that you think of what we have described. After you think of it with certitude, you must take it into yourself. That truth must grow within you. You must think, using that truth.

The Giver of Immeasurable Grace, the One who is Incomparable Love, the Perfect Completion is *al-hamdu lillāh. Al-hamdu lillāh.* He is the Complete One. All praise belongs to Him. The One to whom all praise belongs, the Merciful One, gives us the grace. He gives us love. This is how you have to remember. This is how you have to love Him. This is how you have to worship. This is how you have to pray.

Every breath must remember Him. To place your intention upon Him is to worship Him. To place your intention upon Him, to focus upon Him, to remember Him, to praise Him through His names every moment—without holding anything equal to Him—is worship. You must do it like this. Is that enough? *Ah.*

May God protect us. May the Rahmān, the Most Compassionate, bestow His mercy upon us. May He give us faith, that wisdom and certitude, and that explanation. *Yā Rabbal-'ālamīn*, O Merciful One, may You protect and sustain us. *Al-hamdu lillāh*.

All praise belongs to You. O Merciful Rahmān, O Most Merciful One, O Most Wealthy One, O Compassionate One, O Rahmān, *al-hamdu lillāh*, *yā* Rabbal-'ālamīn, all praise belongs to You. *Āmīn. Āmīn. Yā* Rabbal-'ālamīn.

The Secret of Direct Worship
June 12, 1983

At all times and in every point, everything in our lives is a mess except for God. Everything is upside down. Every section in our lives is a mess. Except for God Himself, our minds, our bodies, our thoughts, and our desires are like this. As soon as something comes, there is a mess.

If you have no food, there is a mess in your mind. If you have too much food, there is a mess in your stomach—if you do not have a bowel movement, there is a mess in your stomach. If you cannot get what you are thinking of, there is a mess in your head. Your entire life is like that. The heart of every human being in God's creation contains wisdom, ignorance, mind, desires, truth, falsehood, good, evil, and many similar things that torment us.

My love you, jeweled lights of my eyes. We begin by saying, "All praise and glory belong only to Allāh." As the foundation for everything we do, we begin by saying, "All praise and glory belong only to Allāh."

When we address Allāh as the Giver of Immeasurable Grace, the One who is Incomparable Love, the Bestower of Inexhaustible Divine Wealth, that is the truth. There is no limit to His grace. No matter what is taken from it, His Divine Wealth remains exactly the same.

He is the Giver of Immeasurable Grace. He is the One who is Incomparable Love. There is no one in all creation who gives love as He does. There is no parallel or equal to His love. He gives boundless love to all lives, to all creations—the grasses, the weeds, the trees, the bushes, the ants that crawl, the birds that fly, human beings, animals. And because He also created *shaitān*, He helps him as well. He fulfills his requests as well. Such is the state of love in which God exists. He is the Giver of Immeasurable Grace, the One who is Incomparable Love. There is no equal to His love.

Why should we find fault with the One who bestows grace like that, who bestows love like that?

When illnesses and diseases arise from our own ignorance and lack of wisdom, we blame God. We find fault with Him. This is how our faith exists. He is the Giver of Immeasurable Grace, the One who is Incomparable Love, the Bestower of Inexhaustible Divine Wealth. He is the One who can grant us everything we ask for. Yet we blame the Wealthy One who gives us everything.

Why? What do we ask for? Does anyone ask God for only one thing at a time? No. Before he contacts God, he thinks of one thing. When he gets there, he asks for four hundred trillion ten thousand things—one after the other, after the other! He does not ask for just one thing. So many *reels* are running. So is God a mess or this the mess?

It is his mind.

We claim that God does not give us what we ask for. God has said, "Take what you want and go." God looks at us and says, "All right. Here it is. Take it. Simply make your decision. Choose what you want: This is My *dunyā*. This is *rahmah*, compassionate grace. This is maya. This is grace. These are the treasures. They are inexhaustible. These are the treasures of *'ilm*, the treasures of grace, the treasures of *gnānam*, the treasures of maya, the treasures of the *dunyā*. They are all for you. Everything is here. Just choose what you want." God says this and puts everything in front of us.

He puts the *dunyā*, the *ākhirah*, and the *awwal*—the physical world, the kingdom of God, and the beginning—in front of us. He puts heaven and hell, the *'arsh*, the *kursī*, and the *qalam*—the throne of God, the eye of wisdom, and the pen that writes destiny—in front of us. The good and the evil are all there.

"Take whatever you need," He says.

However, because of man's greed, it all glitters. Everything sparkles. Man does not focus only on one thing—he takes that, he takes this, and he takes another. After he grabs it all, he cannot carry it.

"Very well," says God. "Pick it up and take it with you!" Man cries because he cannot carry it. Because he cannot carry it on his back, he tries to put it on his head. When he fails, he cries. He asks for a title, and then cries because he cannot carry it. He asks for money, and then cries because he cannot carry it. He asks for a woman, and then cries because he cannot carry her. He asks for a house and a life, and then cries because he cannot manage them. He asks for a child, and then cries because he cannot educate the child or bring it to a good state. He asks for a mat, and then cries because he cannot clean it before he goes to sleep.

He cries about everything he has asked for and received.

Is that God's fault? Man does not ask only for one thing, he asks for ten billion things! When God gives them to him and he tries to pick them up, he cries. That is not God's fault.

God has said, "God will bountifully and exactly grant the request of he who asks." Man chose what he wanted, and now he cries about his life.

The snake was once very beautiful—before it raised its

hood. It looked like a flower garland, except the snake was even more lovely. When God gazed at them, He saw that one was a flower garland and the other was a snake. Both of them were fragrant. He said, "Long ago, I gave the snake a fragrance and I gave the flower a fragrance. They were both fragrant. But the snake possesses poison and the flower possesses thorns. Choose what you will."

Man chose the snake. He wore it as a necklace until the inherent nature of the snake manifested itself. Even if man chooses the flower, the thorns will prick his hand if he picks it up without wisdom. Either the poison or the thorns can affect him. He has to understand how he needs to pick up the flower. He has to understand how he needs to pick up the snake, or whether he has to beat it off or kill it. If he picks it up, he has to understand how to extract the poison. His work is to know both. He has to understand and learn.

Until he does understand, man blames God. If something happens to his body, if he experiences a pain or an ache or thinks of something negative, he calls God a sinner. This is what we call our Creator! He is the Giver of Immeasurable Grace, the One who is Incomparable Love, the Bestower of Inexhaustible Divine Wealth. He gives you whatever you need. This is the kind of Lord Allāh is.

He provides boundlessly without diminishing. This is the One Thing in your *qalb*, your innermost heart, that provides boundlessly without diminishing. It is a Treasure of grace, a Thing of grace. It is an ever-complete Thing. Take as much as you want! It will never diminish. It does not diminish.

You are the one who diminishes it. If your pot is small, your wealth will be small. If your *qalb* is cracked, everything you put into it will be cracked. If your *qalb* is correct, even if you take only a drop, that drop will fill your *qalb*.

We make many mistakes. God does not make any mistakes. However, *my love you*, jeweled lights of my eyes. This is the meaning of the Giver of Immeasurable Grace. This is the meaning of His love. This is the meaning of His treasures. He has given us the earth, the sky, light, eyes, ears, sound, breath, speech, beauty, clothing, a body, a place to live.

What has He not given us? He has given us this vast world. He has put the *zīnah*, the beauty, into your beautiful face. He has given you wisdom.

We have to use what He has given. We need to know where to use each thing—in which section. If we use it as it was meant to be used, there will be no complications. If we fail to use it correctly, there will be problems.

If we squeeze a lemon, the sourness will come if it is squeezed up to its limit. It has a different taste when it is squeezed too much—acid will come from the lemon peel and the taste will be different. A different taste will come and a different nature will be brought into the juice. Is that the fault of the lemon?

Life is just like this. If we take what comes correctly with wisdom, then life will be life and the taste will be the taste. If we fail to squeeze the juice correctly out of our lives with wisdom, then life will be hell. Life will be hell, it will be sad.

If we undertake a proper journey with wisdom, it will be a journey and the way will be short, that path in life will be short. The straight path is short. Unless we correctly draw up the map with wisdom, our path will be long, long, long, and roundabout. We will feel tired. If we do not manage our lives clearly or walk correctly, we will make our path long.

My love you. Our own mistakes will return to us. We have generated most of the mistakes in our lives.

We say that all praise belongs to God. That is fine. Some people praise God with flowery words. But it is not consistent with my wisdom to think that God joyously accepts that praise with a smile. All praise and glory already belong to Him. Do we think God becomes great, esteemed, and glorious because we say He is great, esteemed, and glorious? We say these things and we praise Him with our own lips. Yet I believe that He is not someone who loves praise. He is not someone who loves greatness or titles. Is there anyone, anyone at all, in this *dunyā*, in *'ālamul-arwāh*, or in the eighteen thousand universes who is capable of praising even His kingdom?

Allāh is a secret. He is a mystery. He is a Slave to the slave. He does not collect praise. To the exalted, He is the One who is more exalted. To the learned, he is the One who has learned more. To the unlearned, He is the One who has learned less. To the poor, He is the One who has less. To the rich, He is the One who has more. To those who are praised and glorified, He is beyond all praise and glory. To those who are lowly and poor, He is more lowly and poor.

To someone who says, "There is nothing like me!" God shows him and says to him, "There is absolutely nothing like Me." To someone who says, "There is no one as low as me," God will be lower. What praise and glory can be given to such a Lord?

The flowery praise we give to Him is in our mouths. The taste of the praise we give to Him remains in our mouths. He does not blissfully accept the title. He is happier when you hit Him. If you find fault with your Creator, He is happier.

At one moment, we say, "Allāh! O my Creator! Rabbal-'ālamīn! Lord of the Universes! O Rahmān! O Most Compassionate! Bless me! You have helped me so much. You have done so many things for me!"

At the next moment, we say, "*Adā*![7] You blind God! Do You have eyes? Are You just a statue? Are You just a form? Who has ever said anything good about You? You have no ears, no eyes, no nose!"

---

7 *adā, aday* disrespectful interjections used to address an inferior

This is what we say the next second. In one moment man will praise Him, and in the very next moment he will accuse Him, saying everything that comes to his mouth.

That is why God does not accept man's praise or blame. He accepts neither praise nor blame. He is not happy when He is praised nor is He sad when He is criticized, when we say, "*Adā*, God! Tell me, don't You have eyes? O God, tell me, where are You?"

He says, "You sometimes speak as if God is lower than you. If I were to accept your words when you say that I am either above you or below you, I could become angry. Instead, I will praise you when you praise Me and just look at you when you blame Me. If I blamed you, you would suffer.

"So if you speak of Me, just criticize Me, and say whatever you want to say. I will not be angry. I will not feel hurt. Just say, *Adā, adā, adā, adā, adā, adā, adā,* when you speak to Me. I am happy when you address Me with *aday*."

People say, "*Adā, adā,* O God. *Adā,* Allāh. Where have You gone? *Adā,* Rahmān. *Adā,* Rahīm." The *adā* comes. In Tamil, people say, "*Adā,* O God, where did You go? Where were You? Were You outside or inside?"

I too have said this. At one time, I spoke like this. I did ask forgiveness for it. Whether He forgave me I do not know. I will know after I go. I will only know when I go. *My love you*, jeweled lights of my eyes.

All that we see in our lives are our own mistakes. Only after we correct those mistakes will our lives be good—they will be heaven. Then our lives will be sweet, happy, and heavenly.

Until we understand both sides, we will be in hell here. Hell means our own qualities and affairs. The *'adhāb*, the punishment, of hell means the form of the thoughts we think—the evil form of our thoughts. Those are the snakes, the scorpions, the demons, the ghosts, the blood-sucking vampires, the *kāli*, the *vairavan*, and the legions of devils. That is the *'adhāb* we will face tomorrow in hell.

My love you, jeweled lights of my eyes! Are we now in heaven or hell? Brother? Are you in hell or in heaven?

The man who is being addressed does not answer.

BAWA MUHAIYADDEEN ☮ *insisting, as everyone laughs* Ay! Tell us!

THE MAN *speaking softly and thoughtfully* I am in hell.

BAWA MUHAIYADDEEN ☮ Yes. Are you not experiencing the *'adhāb*? Every person is being pinched here, pinched there, pinched here, pinched there, being bitten and bitten every second.

Your mind is creating so many kinds of *musībāt*, calamities. It is bringing you the world. It bites you every time it brings you something from the *dunyā*. It bites you again when it brings you the next thing; it bites you again when it brings you the one after that; and it bites you again when it brings you the one after that. The mind is generating the *'adhāb* for man every second. He thinks they are just desires and attachments—but those are actually poisonous creatures! Everything to which he is connected comes to bite him.

Every section we have nurtured is coming to bite us. Money is coming to bite us. Land is coming to bite us. The sky is coming to bite us. The dog is coming to bite us. Desire is coming to bite us. The cat is coming to bite us. The rat is coming to bite us. The snake is coming to bite us.

Each creature is a quality. Every thought comes to bite and bite and bite and bite us. We suffer the *'adhāb* for each one and become weaker. As one bites us and another comes to bite us and another, we become unable to even smile. As the mind comes, as each thought comes to bite us in the *qalb*, our happiness quickly departs. That is hell.

We experience the *'adhāb* here in the body. The body is suffering here in this *bahr*, this sea, of hellfire—we are already experiencing the *'adhāb*. We will suffer there in the same fire—it is the same fire. Everything that happens here takes form to bite us there.

Our thoughts will take form, the *nafs* will take form, and desire will take a shape. Anger, lust, hatred, greed, fanaticism, envy, pride, praise, honors, awards, falsehood, jealousy, vengeance, and revenge will take form. The things you are thinking now will take form and bite you then. They are making you suffer here even now.

It is this section that will become the poisonous creatures that will take form and implement the *'adhāb* for you tomorrow in hell—these qualities.

Has Allāh placed anything else there? Only what we do to ourselves will be there. Precious jeweled lights of my eyes, each of our children must reflect with wisdom. There is no hell there. We are building hell here. There is no heaven there. We are building heaven here. There is no good and evil reserved for us there. God has already given us absolutely everything— good and evil are already here.

Will you obtain good or evil? It depends on what you build—that will be the house built there for you. Will it be hell or heaven? It will be the hell or the heaven we have sought. Judgment is here. The witness is here. Conscience[8] is the witness. Justice, wisdom, the truth of Allāh, and the point are here. It is all here. Profit and loss are here—they are the things we have sought. People say there are swings awaiting us in a heaven of beautiful palaces. The heaven of the *'arsh* is here. As a result of this, what we seek and cling to here is the place we will reach there.

Allāh has said, "*Yā* Muhammad, without you I would not

---

8 conscience   In Tamil, the conscience is called *mana-sadchi*, the heart's witness.

have created anything. I have given everything to Adam☮ and to the children of Adam☮ except for the one thing I have kept for Myself. I gave all ninety-nine of My *wilāyāt* to them. I have kept only one and that one is in My hand. I have given humankind three thousand blessings and ninety-nine *wilāyāt*. My actions, conduct, and characteristics, hell and heaven are within them. Their actions and conduct, the things they seek and the things they do not seek, profit and loss, heaven, and the underworld are all within them."

Other than what they have sought here, where else would hell be? Will the questions be asked in this *qabr*, this grave here, or will the grave be transported there? Will the questions be asked in the cemetery here, or there?

The questions will be in the *qabr* here. Every day there are questions. The *malā'ikah*, the angels, are listening and recording what we do, are they not? They hear every breath we take. The questions of the grave are being asked here now. We must give the correct answers to these questions. We must have *sabūr*. We must be strong. We must do *taubah*, we must feel remorse. If we make a mistake, we must do *taubah*. If we do something good, we must say, "O Allāh, I praise You."

We must ask God for a way in which to do no evil.

We must ask God for the strength to do good and to do our duties. We must ask Allāh, saying, "Our eyes have become completely blind! O God, open my eyes to the straight path! Maya, darkness, the hypnotic delusions, hell, and desire have blinded our eyes. Take away this forgetfulness and open my eyes." This is what we must ask.

The harbor is here, the grave is here—in the *qalb*. This is where the *rūh*, the soul, is buried, where Allāh is buried, where the *rusul*, the messengers, are buried, where the Qur'ān is buried, where everything in the *'ālam* and *'ālamul-arwāh*, this world and the world of pure souls, is buried.

The soul is here. Everything has been buried here in the

qalb. This is where the questions will be asked and where the answers will be given. The guilt and the innocence are here inside each individual. Everything every person has to know is here.

The witness is also here. The inquiry, the judgment, the questions, and whether the case is won or lost abide within each person. Every individual will know his own defeats and losses.

Here in the world you can tell a lie and win your case. Are you going to win your case in the grave by lying to the angels? You can win in the *dunyā* by lying to people. Are you going to win in the grave like that? You cannot win like that in the grave. You can lie to the people in the world. In the grave, the angels will be there.

At Qiyāmah, at Judgment Day, each part and every faculty of your body will speak. The eyes will speak of what they saw. The ears will speak of what they heard. The nose will speak of what it smelled. The twenty-eight letters [of which your body is formed] will speak. They are the witnesses. They will relay all the sounds, noises, voices, and forms in pictures. They have all been recorded. The *reels* are there. You cannot bear false witness there. Everything we have done, the house we have built, hell, and heaven will be there.

Jeweled lights of my eyes, because it is like that, we should never act for the world—for the respect of the world, for the praise of the world. We must never worship for the sake of the world, pray the five daily prayers for the sake of the world, speak in such a way as to obtain praise from the world, or study, sing, and dance for the sake of the world. The world will not come with you.

The world will not come with you nor will the body come with you. Your relatives will not come with you nor will your parents come with you. These crazy people will not come with you.

Nothing in this demonic world will get past the cemetery.

There, however, the good and the evil we have sought, the witness, the justice, the *rūh*, and the angels within us could come with us as witnesses. They are the witnesses. None of the others will come with us. We should think of this.

We must realize every word we speak: Am I cheating the world or am I cheating myself? Am I harming the world or am I harming myself? Am I earning the world or am I earning Allāh's treasures? This is what we must think of.

Who is the witness for all this?

My life has been very long. When I was with my Shaikh, I got into mischief. I was very naughty. I bit people and pinched them. I did a lot of that and got into a lot of mischief. One day when I was rolling down the mountainside, I fell into a pond and became tangled in the trailing stems of the lotus plants. In that pond were many crocodiles.

I was trapped by the lotus stems and ten or twelve crocodiles surrounded me, yet they did not attack me. They only circled around me. I was in the center, in the water. I was little. I was extremely mischievous, still small. I can remember it even now.

My Shaikh had seen me rolling down the mountain and was running towards me. I was young and small like 'Aisha' here. When my Shaikh came to get me out, the crocodiles scattered. He entered the pond and carried me out. I had some cuts and bruises from the thorns and stones that had struck me when I rolled down the mountain.

My Shaikh picked a few plants and put them on the cuts. I still remember that, even after all this time. The *reels*, the recordings, are there. I can still see those plants, I can still remember them now. I can still see this even after so much time has gone by.

The *reels* have not disappeared. Nothing has disappeared. We can see those things. The *reels* come into our dreams or they come into a moment of reflection or they come into our thoughts or they come at a time of sadness or worry.

A recollection can come when we are sad. A remembrance can come when we worry. The *reels* can come into a dream or a memory. The *reels* can come at a moment of distress. Only you can see them, others cannot.

We can see this from our own experiences.

Jeweled lights of my eyes, we must think of all this. We are the witnesses. We are on trial—either we are guilty or we are innocent. We are also the judges.

Should we make our decision by siding with the mind or by siding with the truth? We contain both sides. The mind is within us. It deceives us with a huge smile. The truth is within us. The *qalb*, the innermost heart, too is within us, yet the *qalb* does not deceive us, it is constantly sad and sorrowful, thinking, *Why is he acting like that*?

The *qalb* too can smile, with happiness, except that it does not act deceptively like the mind. It is waiting to embrace with love. The deception of the mind takes various forms like a dog or a cat prepared to pounce, thinking, *How can we finish him off*? This is what the mind does.

These two sides—truth and the mind—bear witness, and you give the judgment. Are you going to favor the *qalb* or the mind?

The *qalb* looks old and worn out. Over here, the mind looks like a young and beautiful witness. If you favor youth and beauty when you give the judgment, the mess will be yours. It is your life. You can abandon the truth and favor the mind, saying, "You win, the truth loses." You have to give the judgment. We have to think of each thing in our lives like this.

My love you, jeweled lights of my eyes. The five daily prayers, *'ibādah*, and fasting are also like this. We do not engage in them for the sake of the other people, the village, the relatives, or the religions. The food we give to the poor, our charity, our *sadaqah*, our fast, our hajj, our worship, our five daily prayers, the duties we do, our actions, and our conduct are done for our own sake.

They are not for the sake of others. We will not be questioned for their sake. Other people are not going to bear witness tomorrow at Judgment as to the good and evil we may have done, or the good heaven we may get. We have to do this ourselves. This is our own undertaking—it belongs to us as our birthright.

It is our birthright to worship the Lord who created us. Our wealth is to make Him clearly evident within ourselves and then to obtain His wealth. Your work is to bow down before Him in reverence, and if you fast for His sake, to think of the reason you are alive, to feel for the poor, to distribute food, and give *sadaqah* to them.

That is a lot of work. We must be the proof of good conscience in everything we do. We must have that awe and fear. You must be in awe—Allāh is with you at all times. We must do His duty.

He is the Witness who is with us, greater than all the other witnesses and the angels. He is always watching us. Those who do not see this will keep babbling. Yet Allāh looks at this with *sabūr*. Allāh watches us with *sabūr* all the time—He sees every breath we take.

A person who knows nothing babbles incessantly at the world, saying, "That man is an evil man! This man is a good man! That one over there is an evil man!" while he praises the evil man and attacks the good man. He will make a learned man into an idiot and an idiot into a learned man. He is the evil one.

The Good One will always watch with *sabūr*, without deviating for even a fraction of a second. He exists with *sabūr*. We must truly understand this with *īmān* in our *qalb*s. There is not an atom of time in which He does not watch us. There is nothing He does not know.

> *I praise the One*
> *who knows the frog under the stone,*
> *who provided there a leaf for it to eat,*
> *who provides for all the created lives.*

Moses⊛ sang this song on Mount Sinai. He had gone there to receive the Ten Commandments. When he was at the base of the mountain, he looked for water to give his pregnant wife, Zipporah⊛.

These are small examples, I am not going to tell the entire story, just the point.

He had climbed Mount Sinai and was speaking with Allāh. Moses⊛ thought of his wife, Zipporah⊛, and his attention went to her.

Allāh called him, "Moses! Moses! Moses! Where did you go? Where are you now?" He sent the sound down three times, shouting loudly the third time.

It was only then that Moses⊛ said, "Allāh! I am here. I have been here."

Allāh said, "You were not here. Kick that stone."

Moses⊛ kicked it and the stone cracked open. Under it was small hollow containing a frog and a small amount of water. The frog jumped away with a leaf in its mouth.

Allāh asked him, "What was that, Moses? Did you see it before?"

Moses⊛ replied, "No, Allāh."

"Who provided the water and the leaf? Who provided it?" asked Allāh.

"Only You can do this. You are the One who gave the frog food and water," said Moses⊛.

Then Allāh said, "Would the One who did not forget to give water and food to the frog under the stone beneath your feet forget your Zipporah? That is where you went. You went there, did you not? I called you three times and you were not here."

That was when Moses⊚ sang the song about the frog under the stone.

Allāh is the One who watches us like this, is He not? Our own flaws are making us suffer. When we know for certain that He has given us everything and when we strengthen our *īmān*, elevate our lives, and correct our flaws, we will obtain the victory in our lives and reach heaven.

If we can work together in unity, put an end to the differences and enmities that belong to the mind—and if our brothers and sisters do not have the differences and enmities of the *dunyā*—we will obtain peace. If we dispel the qualities that attack others—the racial and religious divisions, the qualities of color, complexion, and language differences—unity and love will live within us.

When unity and love live within us, hatred, enmity, and turmoil will leave us. When the pride, the deceit, the treachery, and the vengeance that are the qualities of *shaitān* leave us, and when the *sabūr*, the *shukūr*, the *tawakkul*, and the *al-hamdu lillāh* that are the divine qualities of Allāh come to us and make our lives into a flower garden, we will live in unity in that garden. When we realize that God is One, we will obtain His reward in the flower garden of the *dunyā*, living as one family in happiness. We will see that.

Like this, it is our own ignorance that will topple us. If we can separate ourselves from that which separates us from each other, if we can separate ourselves from that which comes to disturb unity, we can attain peace, tranquility, and serenity. We must separate ourselves from that which separates us from each other. Then we are certain to attain truth and peace in our lives.

If we can separate ourselves from being attacked by the anger, the doubt, the suspicion, and the desire that separate each child from his brothers and sisters, our brothers and sisters will not be separate from us. If we can separate ourselves from that which comes to separate us from our brothers and sisters—the evil that disrupts unity—we will not be separate from unity. This is how we must think and act in our lives, precious jeweled lights of my eyes.

The most exalted fast in life is unity. This exalted fast—the genuine qualities of God's kingdom—is the heaven that is the birthright of the one family. This state is paradise. This is the unity that exists in heaven where there are no "other" races, "other" colors, "other" complexions, "other" kinds, "other" gods. There is One God, one family of Adam ☻. There is no other God worthy of worship. We are one family.

There is one place for human beings. There are many places for those who have transformed themselves into animals and beasts—those are the places called hell, *jahannam*. There is one place for *insān*, man, one place for this family.

There are many sections in hell for those who have transformed themselves from *insān* into *hayawānāt*, animals, and snakes. Those are the sections for the *'adhāb*. For those who have changed and become *shaitāns*, there is the *'adhāb*, the torment, of many rebirths. *'Adhāb!* Tormented births!

Let us think of this, jeweled lights of my eyes. We must accept and do everything with clarity in our lives. Because we do the five daily prayers for the sake of God, we must give our *qalbs* to Him. Only He and we understand the witnessing and the truth. Others who stand next to us will not understand the happiness that comes from prayer.

They will not see it. Allāh is the One who can see, and you are the one who can understand. You are the giver and He is the Receiver and He is the Giver and you are the receiver—you are shareholders. You do know that both of you can give and receive, do you not? You know the happiness that comes when He accepts what you give Him and you accept what He gives you. This is worship, this is prayer.

When you give *dharma* or *sadaqah*, charity, to someone, you yourself will know the state of your *qalb* when you give it and the one who accepts it will know the state of his *qalb* when he receives it. Only the two of you know your thoughts.

When you give or receive, it depends upon your state—whether you are doing it as a display, or to make someone happy, or to establish a relationship with someone, or because that person is a blood relative, or because that person is a sibling in the one family, or because you were acting in unity with the qualities of God and the compassion of God.

God sees that. God sees what the two of you are doing. This is why what you give someone either fulfills his needs and makes him happy, or does not fulfill his needs or make him happy.

It is like this for everything we do—it all comes from us. A tree gives the fruit from within itself. A seed gives the tree from within itself. A cow gives the milk from within itself. Each and every creation gives what is within it. A cow gives milk, flesh, and skin from itself. It gives from itself. In happiness and in sorrow, a cow and a goat give their life, their skin, their flesh.

Since they are like that, where should what we give come from? Where should our duty come from when we do something good? We have to open our *qalbs*—we have to give from the *qalb*. The cow and the goat give their lives. We have to open our *qalbs*—split them open—and give love and compassion as One Life to other lives.

If a human being cannot do even as much as a cow, how can he rise higher? If he cannot do even the work of a tree, how can he be called human? It is not possible. The blood of a cow and a goat is transformed into water and the water is transformed into milk. If a human being could change his evil qualities, the world, and his bondage to his blood ties with love, with compassion, with empathy, with equality, peace, and a state of love in his *qalb*; if he could transform his *qalb* into a state of love—he could at least give love as his milk. If he gives love to someone as his milk, he can make him peaceful. The cow transforms its blood. A human being should dispel his evil qualities and at least give love and show compassion. Then he would have peace.

It is like this, precious jeweled lights of my eyes, every one of you! Completely cut off your thoughts and faults in worship, the five daily prayers, *'ibādah*, your search, and your intentions. Open the good paths, accept the good ways and God's qualities, and act accordingly. For the sake of brotherly unity, you must try to grow by teaching, giving, embracing, comforting, and lovingly trusting your brothers and sisters. It is with these qualities that you will obtain the great victory. These are the rewards you will receive, the treasures you will gather. This is the heaven in our lives. These are our good gifts of peace and tranquility.

We can reach the state of being immensely wealthy people. God has told us this.

Each child must understand what we have to do, the commandments we have to follow—God's commandments—and the duties we have to do with open hearts. We have to do this in the state of God's qualities. We have to transform ourselves with His laws of justice. We have to act in a state of justice, living with those who have been born with us.

We have to live with them, gather together with them, associate with them, and relate to them with love, acting with *dānam, nidānam,* and *avadanam*—surrender, balance, and concentration—in this *dunyā*, and with the four qualities of good conduct—*nānam, madam, acham,* and *payippu*, modesty, reserve, respect for others, and fear of wrongdoing. We must stay out of the hands of *shaitān*, and lead our lives with good conduct.

We must act with the qualities of Allāh. We must walk on the path of good conduct, patience, and *sabūr* as demonstrated to us by the messengers, the *ambiyā'*, and the Rasūl ☬, thus obtaining the love of Allāh and loving Him, surrendering to Him, opening our hearts, and giving the wonder that is the *amānah*—the treasure He gave us to hold in trust until our return to Him—as a gift to Him.

We must embrace and hold on to Him, surrendering ourselves to Him, making that surrender become the clarity in our worship as we seek Him in our prayers. This is the most exalted state of wisdom and love. This is the good state of searching for goodness. We need to think of this. Each child must have this intention and act accordingly.

We must think like this: Worshipping God is done without duality. We must establish a direct connection to Him without attributing an associate or an equal to Him. The *qalb* must connect directly to Him, without an associate, a parallel, or an equal. There must be no associate or equal between God and that *qalb*. The *qalb* must make a direct connection without making any other god His equal, without comparing Him to the earth, the sky, the sun, the moon, gold, silver, spirits, or angels. The *qalb* must make a direct connection to Him, connecting to Allāh without using a parallel or an equal.

To connect to Him, to love Him, to trust Him, to have *īmān* in Him, to pray to Him, and to give Him the responsibility with a strong heart is worship. To accept Him directly into the *qalb* without any duality, without any associate, and to give yourself completely to Him is worship. That is true worship, true prayer.

That is the secret of direct worship.

The qualities of many suns, moons, and stars, demons and ghosts, maya and darkness, arrogance and karma, snakes and scorpions, eagles and vultures, peacocks and cuckoos,

The Secret of Direct Worship

crows, dogs and jackals, elephants, cows and goats, horses and donkeys, lions and tigers, and similar beasts may appear in the *qalb* and the mind of man, and those qualities may take various statue forms, golden forms, stone forms, clay forms, and sun forms.

When they are manufactured and worshipped as elephant and cat forms, that is not worship. Those are the forms in man's mind, the forms of maya. That is hell. There is no way a human being can ever worship like that.

Worship means to have a direct connection. Worship is to have a direct, unblemished, unmarked connection with God. Let us think of this. Let us think of this in our lives. *My love you*, jeweled lights of my eyes.

May we think of how to worship this incomparable Lord. The clarity that will come from doing so will be the clarity of our worship, the exaltedness of our lives, the exaltedness of the state we will reach, the birthright of Allāh's paradise, the rewards of paradise that we will receive. May we think of this.

Each child, ask forgiveness for your faults. Turn each breath towards Allāh. Do *taubah*, feel remorse, for your faults. To worship Him, do *tasbīh*, glorify Him.

We must submit each breath in that state. We must ask forgiveness for our faults every day. We must dedicate our worship to Him every day. We must do both: for our faults we must do *taubah*, for our worship we must do *tasbīh*. We must give each breath to Him in *dhikr*. The reward will come from that.

My love you, jeweled lights of my eyes. May you have unchanging unity and love at each moment in time. May you grow in brotherhood. May our family, Allāh's family, grow in this way.

You must live in this state. You must attain your birthright. This is the truth and the wealth and the unity of the family of God's children. May we think of this.

May Allāh help us. May He grant us His *rahmah* and His blessing for this, and protect us.

May He lift us out of this deep pit of the darkness of ignorance, dispel the darkness, and give us Light. May He free us from this karmic hell.

May He transform us and save us from being demons of desire dwelling in the darkness and delusion of the mind, and give us the clarity of the Light of wisdom, truth, and *īmān*.

May He make us act with His qualities, bring us to a fully developed state, and make us complete on His path.

May He embrace us, give us refuge, and feed us with the milk of wisdom, the milk of love, the milk of *gnānam*, the milk of the *'ilm* of His qualities, and protect us with His grace.

Āmīn. Āmīn. As-salāmu 'alaikum wa rahmatullāhi wa barakātuh. Peace be upon you and the compassionate grace and blessings of God.

Salawāt *for Prophet Muhammad* ☮.

As-salāmu 'alaikum.

M. R. Bawa Muhaiyaddeen (May God be pleased with him)

The words of Muhammad Raheem Bawa Muhaiyaddeen☺ reveal the Sufi path of esoteric Islām: that the human being is uniquely created with the faculty of wisdom, enabling him to trace himself back to his Origin—Allāh, the Creator and Cherisher of all the Universes who exists in Oneness with all lives—and to surrender to that Source, leaving the One God, the Truth, as the only reality in his life. This is the original intention of the purity that is Islām.

Bawa Muhaiyaddeen☺ spoke endlessly of this Truth through parables, discourses, songs, and stories, all pointing the way to return to God. Over fifteen thousand hours of this ocean of knowledge were recorded.

People of all ages, religions, classes, backgrounds, and races flocked to hear and be near him; he interacted compassionately and lovingly with all of them, opening his heart to them equally, regardless of who they were. Presidents of countries and fakirs from the streets, the proud and the humble, the high-ranking and the low-ranking, the ordinary and the extraordinary, the extremely poor and the extremely rich all sat side by side in his presence.

An extraordinary being, Bawa Muhaiyaddeen ☺ taught from experience, having traversed the path and returned, divinely aware—sent back to exhort all who yearn for the experience of God to discover the inner wisdom that is the path of surrender to that One.

Bawa Muhaiyaddeen ☺ did not tell us much about his life, although there were rare moments when he spoke to those gathered around him of certain memories.

What we know is that he was first sighted by spiritual seekers at the edge of the jungle near the pilgrimage town of Kataragama in what was then known as the island country of Ceylon. A man we know only as Pariari and a few others from the town of Kokuvil caught brief, unforgettable glimpses of him there.

The tiny island that is shaped like a teardrop falling from the tip of southern India is a place known for its legendary as well as its sacred geography. Adam's Peak in the center of the island is said to have retained the imprint created by the impact of Adam's foot from when he first touched the earth after being cast out of the Garden of Eden.

Referred to in the ancient text of the *Ramayana* as Lanka, it was the site of Princess Sita's captivity by her abductor, Ravana, the evil demon-king of Lanka. The *Ramayana* contains details of the battlefields where the armies of her husband, Prince Rama, fought the armies of the demon-king, and describes the groves of exotic herbs dropped by Hanuman, the monkey-king who helped Prince Rama rescue his wife.

When the island was called the Isle of Serendib, the voyage of Sinbad was described in *The Thousand and One Nights*. Medieval Arabs and Persians made regular pilgrimages to Adam's Peak. The fourteenth century Arab traveler and scholar Ibn Batutah made that pilgrimage.

(May God be pleased with him)

Legends record the visit of the Qutb ☺ who after visiting Adam's Peak meditated for twelve years in what came to be known as the hermitage shrine of Daftar Jailani that lies at the edge of a precipitous granite cliff in the south central portion of the island, a site that has become a place of saintly visitation and mystical meditation.

Living in that land of legends, those seekers from Kokuvil recognized Bawa Muhaiyaddeen ☺ as a uniquely mystical being when they began to interact with him, begging him to teach them. He had lived peacefully alone in the jungle for so long that he had almost forgotten human speech. Gradually, he began to speak with those seekers.

Telling those seekers that God was the only Teacher, he consented only to study side by side with them. Working long hours in the rice fields as a farmer by day, he spoke and sang to them of his experiences of God in the evenings. Eventually, he and that small group of seekers from Kokuvil built an ashram in Jaffna, a town in the northern tip of the country.

Travel was difficult in that small country, yet the refuge of his presence was irresistible. As more and more people came to know about him and to hear him sing and speak of God, many of them began to invite him to stay in their homes. Among those people were Dr. Ajwad Macan-Markar and his wife Ameen Macan-Markar who lived in the city of Colombo. Bawa Muhaiyaddeen ☺ told them it would not be easy: that he was like a tree upon which many birds needed to take shelter. If he was to agree to stay at their home, they would also have to accommodate these birds. He warned them that there could be many at times. Dr. Ajwad and his wife did not hesitate to agree to open their home to all who wished to accompany him. After that, Bawa Muhaiyaddeen ☺ always stayed at their home when he was in Colombo. For forty years Bawa Muhaiyaddeen ☺ spent his time with those seekers until 1971.

In *The Tree That Fell to the West,*[9] Bawa Muhaiyaddeen ☺ tells us:

> Before I arrived at 46th Street in Philadelphia for my first visit, Bob Demby, Carolyn Secretary, Zoharah Simmons, and some others sitting here arranged for me to come.
>
> They formed a society for that purpose, to invite me here. I did not come to Philadelphia with the idea of establishing a fellowship. There is only one Fellowship and that is Allāh's. There is only one family and one Fellowship. We are all the children of Adam ☺, and Allāh is in charge of that Fellowship.

After that first visit, Bawa Muhaiyaddeen ☺ went back and forth between Philadelphia and what by then had been renamed Sri Lanka until 1982, when he stayed in the United States until December 1986.

In these distressing times, his words are increasingly recognized as representing the original intention of Islām which is the purity of the relationship between man and God as explained by all the prophets of God, from Adam, Noah, Abraham, Ishmael, Moses, David, Jesus, and Muhammad, may the peace of God be upon them, who were all sent to tell and retell mankind that there is one and only One God, and that this One is their Source—attainable, and awaiting the return of each individual soul.

---

9 Muhaiyaddeen ☺, Bawa. *The Tree That Fell to the West*. Philadelphia: Fellowship Press, 2003. Print.

Glossary

The following traditional supplications in Arabic are used throughout the text:

- ☺ *sallAllāhu 'alaihi wa sallam,* may the blessings and peace of Allāh be upon him, is used following Prophet Muhammad, Rasūlullāh, the Messenger of Allāh ☺.
- ☺ *'alaihis-salām,* peace be upon him, is used following the name of a prophet, a wife of a prophet, or an angel.
- ☺ *radiyAllāhu 'anhu* or *anhā,* may Allāh be pleased with him or her, is used following the name of a companion of the Prophet Muhammad ☺, the *aqtāb,* or an exalted saint.

Unless otherwise noted, the glossary words are Tamil, a Dravidian language whose origins in antiquity are unknown.

Although the glossary has been assembled by editors and translators over the years, a majority of the explanations and definitions have come directly from Bawa Muhaiyaddeen ☺.

Pronunciation Key

The non-Arabic and non-Tamil reader of this book will encounter unknown words and names. We have tried to make them as simple as possible to pronounce.

While there are standard ways of transliterating Arabic letters into Roman script, there is no standard system of transliterating Tamil. Thus, we have not adopted any system in its entirety, but are indebted to many.

We have simplified the consonants—for the typical English speaking person, it would not be particularly helpful to distinguish between the two types of s or h or t in Arabic or the two types of t or the three types of n or l in Tamil.

> dh in Arabic is pronounced like the th in then
> kh in Arabic is pronounced like the ch in the Scottish loch
> gn is pronounced like the ng in king or like the ñ in the Spanish word *mañana*
> k has been variously transliterated as k or h or g, because its sound is dependent upon its position in the Tamil word
> th (a confusing and inconsistently applied legacy Tamil transliteration that has come down to us from the German) has been simplified throughout as t or d, depending on its position in the Tamil word

Both Arabic and Tamil have long and short vowels: the long vowels have been indicated by long marks in most cases. Thus, in Arabic and Tamil (except where noted):

a	as in agree for Tamil; as in either agree or apple for Arabic, depending on placement
ā	as in father for Tamil; as above with a lengthening of sound for Arabic
i	as in pin
ī	as in pique
u	as in pull
ū	as in rule
o	as in sock
ō	as in ore

Glossary

e	as in end
ē	as in they
ai	as in aisle except at the end of a word, where it is generally as in day, for Tamil. In Arabic it may sound either like aisle or day, depending on the letter preceding it.

Any good transliteration system, of course, needs to be logically consistent. However, the idiosyncrasies of both languages must be considered; a few well-placed exceptions serve to clarify a sound that would otherwise be mangled. For instance, *nāi* (dog—pronounced as in high) could not be spelled *nāy* without causing confusion, even though that is what the Tamil spelling would seem to indicate.

acham   fear (of wrongdoing)
āchāris   Hindu teachers, priests
adā, aday   disrespectful interjections used to address inferiors
'adhāb   punishment
agnānam   lack of wisdom, ignorance
aiyō   an interjection expressing surprise or dismay
al-ākhirah   the kingdom of God
'alam   world
'ālamul-arwāh   the world of pure souls
al-hamdu lillāh   all praise is due to God
'ālim   a Muslim scholar
Allāh   God
amānah   the treasure held in trust
ambiyā'   prophets
āmīn   may it be so
anbu   love
angam   the body
appā, apapapapā   an interjection expressing surprise
aqtāb   (pl.) of Qutb ☺
'arsh   the throne of God
as-hāb   followers

117

'asr   the afternoon prayer
as-salāmu 'alaikum   peace be upon you
as-salāmu 'alaikum wa rahmatullāhi wa barakātuh   peace be upon you and the compassion and blessings of God
asūras   evil giants in Hindu and Buddhist mythology
āvi   breath
al-awwal   the beginning

bahr   sea

dānam, nidānam, and *avadānam*   surrender, balance, and concentration
daulat   wealth
dharma   charitable duty
dhikr   The remembrance of God; of the many *dhikrs*, the most exalted *dhikr* is, "*Lā ilāha illAllāhu:* There is nothing other than You, (O God). Only You are Allāh." All *dhikrs* relate to His *wilāyāt* or His actions, but this *dhikr* points to Him and to Him alone.
dunyā   world

gnāna   wise
gnānam   wisdom, divine wisdom
gnāni   a man of wisdom
Guru   Teacher
Guru Nādan   a Guru who is a great Master

hayāh   life
hayawān, (pl) *hayawānāt*   animal(s)

'ibādah   worship or service to God performed with a melting heart
'ilm   wisdom, wisdom of the divine
īmān   faith in God, certitude, and determination
Īmān-Islām   Perfect certitude and purity of faith in Allāh; the state of the spotlessly pure heart which contains

Allāh's Holy Qur'ān, His divine radiance, His divine wisdom, His truth, His prophets, His angels, and His laws. When the resplendence of Allāh is seen as the completion within this pure heart of man, that is Īmān-Islām. When the complete, unshakable faith of this pure heart is directed towards the One who is Completeness and is made to merge with that One; when that heart trusts only in Him and worships only Him, accepting Him as the only perfection and the only One worthy of worship—that is Īmān-Islām.

insān   man
'ishā'   the night prayer
Islām   purity

jahannam   the lowest hell

kāli   a demon
kubēras   immensely wealthy, malevolent dwarves in Hindu and Buddhist mythology
kursī   Allāh's seat in the forehead between the eyes; the eye of wisdom between the physical eyes in the center of the forehead
lā ilāha illAllāh   There is nothing other than You, O God; You are God.
lebbay   the caretaker at the mosque

madam   reserve
maghrib   the post-sunset prayer
malā'ikah   the angels
mana-sādchi   the heart's witness, conscience
maruda   a jujube tree
mastān   someone who loves God to the extent of being intoxicated by that love
maunam   silence
maut   death

Muchudar   the Triple Flame
munivar   Hindu ascetic
musībāt   calamities

nabī   prophet
nafs   the self
nambōl   Hindu teacher, priest
nānam, madam, acham, payippu   modesty, reserve, respect for others, fear of wrongdoing
Nūr   Light

odukkam   cessation, disappearance
ōsay   a compelling vocal sound that comes as a summons

panjacharam   the five letters
panīchay   a fruit tree
payippu   fear of wrongdoing
Pērarivu   the seventh level of wisdom
pillay   child
poygnānam   false wisdom
pūjāri   Hindu priests
pūjās   Hindu religious ceremonies
pulavar   poet

qabr   a grave
qalam   the pen that writes destiny
qalb   the innermost heart
Qiyāmah   the Day of Resurrection, the Day of Judgment
qudrah   power
Qutb ☺   The one who is endowed with the power of the Light of grace-awakened Discerning Wisdom that dawned from the throne of God and that investigates, understands, and analyzes everything in the eighteen thousand universes and beyond. Through this inner analysis, the darkness of evil is dispelled and the beauty of

goodness is made clear and radiant. The Qutb☺ is sent by Allāh, through His grace and mercy, to reawaken mankind's faith in God and to establish certitude in our hearts. He is the wondrous embodiment and illustration of *īmān,* absolute faith in God, in all three worlds.

Qutbiyyah   the state of the Qutb☺

rahmah   compassionate grace
rākshidas   evil giants in Hindu and Buddhist mythology
rasūl, (pl) *rusul*   messenger
rūh   the soul

sabūr, shukūr, tawakkul, al-hamdu lillāh   inner patience, gratitude, trust in God, giving all praise to God
sadaqah   charitable giving
sajdah   the prostration in prayer
sannyāsi   a wandering ascetic
Sayyid   Master
shaikh   teacher
shaitān(s)   satan(s)
sharī'ah   the law
shart   rule, right condition, right way
shukūr   gratitude
sīmān   wealthy man
subh   pre-dawn prayer
Sufi   A Sufi exists in the absolute silence of Light within God. He prays with God as God. He performs 43,242 prostrations to God each day. His every breath, every intention, every thought goes out to unite with God. His heart is open and melting with love. He does not harm anyone or kill anything. He feels the suffering of others as his own. He does not belong to any one race or religion. He lives in a state of unity with all lives. He does not dance or take intoxicants. His sustenance is God.
Sufism   the practices undertaken by a Sufi

sūrah form
swami, *swāmiyār* guru, teacher

takbīr *Allāhu akbar,* God is greater; a phrase repeated in the formal prayers with each change of position
tambi younger brother
tasbīh glorifying God
tāttān grandfather
taubah an act of repentence
tawakkul trust in God
tondar a devoted servant or slave

udal, porul, āvi body, possessions, breath
ummah followers, community
ūnjal a swing

vairavan Hindu dog-deity
vanakkam prayer, worship, greetings
vangam a swiftly moving ship
veruhu firewood
vīna a stringed musical instrument
vingnānam scientific wisdom

wahi revelation
walī saint
wilāyah (pl) *wilāyāt* the miraculous duty(ies) and action(s) of God

yā O (used as a respectful form of address)
yā Rabbal-'ālamīn O Lord and Cherisher of All the Universes

zīnah beauty

INDEX

Passim denotes that the references are not to be found on all of the listed pages; e.g., 24-29 *passim* would be used where the reference is on pages 24, 25, 27, and 29.

A

'adhāb (punishment), 95–97, 105
age of twelve, meaning of the, 39–40
Allāh (God)
    he who has accepted—lacks nothing, 37
    looks with *sabūr*, 102
    See also God
angels in the grave, 98–99
animals, those who have transformed themselves into, 105
ant
    hill, 13–20 *passim*
    language, 11–13, 16–17
    a man smaller than an, 9-12, 16-19 *passim*
Ant Man, 4–5, 10–12
atom bombs, escape from the, 16
Awareness, 71-76 *passim*, 81-82

B

Bawa Muhaiyaddeen ☺ and his Shaikh, Hammad ☺, 100
birds will come to the tree of the Guru, 58–60
birthright, 102, 105
book
    is stamped according to your duty, 54-59 *passim*, 63
    knowledge, 36
    learning, 69, 78
    secret, 70-75 *passim*, 82-83

book (*continued*)
    uncompromised account, 70-71, 83
breaths, 80

C

church, can God be seen in a, 78–79
cicada calls the rain, 20–22
city will prosper, 58–59
clarity in our worship, 108–110
cobra with a gem in its mouth, 51-53
Commandments, Ten, 38
connection to God, 108–109
Conscience, 97
correct yourself, 60–63
cow gives its life, 106–107
crocodiles surround Bawa Muhaiyaddeen ☺, 100

D

darkness, dispel the, 46–47
demons, 14–15, 21
destruction of the world, 4, 19–20
disciples, sixty-three, 53–59
duty, do—to the Guru. *See* Guru, serve the

E

eagle cries, 21–22
evils, destroy, 51–52
explanations, understand, 69-77, 81-84 *passim*

F

fault(s)
  ask forgiveness for our, 109
  finding—with God, 90-95
flower
  fragrance in a, 41-42
  garland, 92
forget yourself, 47
forgiveness, ask—for our faults, 109
form, inner—of each person, 77
fragrance in a flower, 41-42
frog under the stone, 103-104
fruit on the tree of the Guru, 57-64 *passim*

G

gem, the real, 48
gnāni (wise man), true, 49, 51
God
  accepts no praise, 95
  asking, 90-91, 98
  the Bestower of Divine Wealth, 89-90
  direct connection to, 108-109
  the Giver of Immeasurable Grace, 89-93 *passim*
  grace of — never diminishes, 92
  house—has built, 14-16
  man blames, 92-95 *passim*
  no one has seen, 19
  the One, 45, 64, 84-85, 94
    who is Incomparable Love, 89-90
  praise of, 93-95
  qualities of, 107-110 *passim*
  the Receiver and the Giver, 105-106
  secret of, 14-15, 18
  umbrella of, 46

God (*continued*)
  worship, 80-82, 108-109
  See also Allāh
good and evil, 97-100 *passim*
grave is in the *qalb*, 98-99
Guru('s)
  do duty to the. *See* Guru, serve the
  is the Lamp, 46-49 *passim*, 55
  learn from the, 69-78
  Nādan, 52-53, 60, 65
  serve the, 45-47, 52-56, 62-66
  speak to the, 73-78
  tree of the, 59
  true, 51
  words, treasure of the, 78, 83
gurus have come to America, 12-13

H

Hammad ☮, Shaikh, 35
happiness from prayer, 105
heart
  book of your, 54
  innermost. *See qalb*
  record in your, 70-72, 75-78
hell, life will be, 93-97 *passim*
hours in a day for prayer, 79-80
house of God, 14-16

I

īmān (absolute faith), understand, 36-39
inner connection to Bawa Muhaiyaddeen ☮, 3-5
Islām, *īmān* is, 36-38

J

Judgment Day, 99
jungle where Bawa Muhaiyaddeen ☮ used to stay, 25-26

K
Kataragama, 25

L
lā ilāha, illAllāh, 50–51
Lamp, Guru is the. *See* Guru is the Lamp
lemon, different tastes of a, 93
leopard and the multitude of monkeys, 27–31
life will be hell, 93-97 *passim*
love
   give, 107
   of God, 90

M
man
   cannot carry things because of his greed, 91
   gives and receives, 105–106
   smaller than an ant, 9–12, 16-20 *passim*
   transformed into animals, 105
   will understand, 81–84
mantra, most exalted, 51
maya, ocean of, 39–40
mess, everything is a—except for God, 89
microphone, check the, 70–71
mind
   bites us, 96
   and the truth, 101
minutes, twenty-five—for prayer, 79–81
mistakes, 61–63, 92–93
mongoose and the snake, 13–15
monkeys, seventy battalions of, 26–31
Moses ☺, 19, 103–104
mosque, can God be seen in a, 78–80

O
ocean, the billowing—of the mind, 39–40
openings
   ten, 38
   twelve, 40
ōsay (a compelling vocal sound), 36

P
Pērarivu (Divine Luminous Wisdom), 17
person, see the inner form of each, 77
place, there is one—for human beings, 105
prayer
   happiness from, 105
   what is, 78–81 *passim*

Q
qabr (grave), questions in the, 98
qalb (innermost heart), 101
   if the—is cracked, 92
   must connect directly to God, 108
   open your, 106–108
Qiyāmah (Judgment Day), 99
questions asked in the grave, 98–102 *passim*
Qutb ☺, the Shaikh of the, 35
Qutbiyyah, 35–37

R
rain, cicada calls the, 20–22
recording in our hearts, 70–72, 75–83 *passim*
reels of our life, 99–101
resplendences, three, 76, 83
restriction of having to correct ourselves, 61–63

root of the connection to the
  Shaikh, 3–4

S

sabūr (inner patience), God looks
  on with, 102
sake, pray for our own, 101-102
secret of God. *See* God, secret of
seedling, grow the—of the connection to the Shaikh, 3–4
Shaikh
  of Bawa Muhaiyaddeen ☺, 35,
    100
  Hammad ☺, 35
  stay with the, 41–42
sharī'ah (the law), 38
ship, swiftly moving—of *īmān*,
  39–40
silence of book learning, 69
sīmān (wealthy man), 36–37
snake
  as a necklace, 91–92
  with a gem in its mouth, 48–53
    passim
  and the mongoose, 13–15
sound will come through the
  connection, 73–76
stamp in the book of the heart,
  54-59 *passim*, 63
Sufism, 37–38

T

Temple of Divine Duty, 63–64
termite house, 13–16
thoughts come to bite, 96–97
titles not needed for God, 10,
  18–19
treasure of the Guru's words, 78,
  83
tree of the Guru
  cutting down the, 59, 64–65
  fruits on the, 60-61

tree of the Guru (*continued*)
  must grow, 55–59
trees in the jungle, 25-27
truth
  accept the, 47, 51
  and the mind, 101

U

umbrella of God, 46
understanding, man will have,
  81–84
unity and love, 104–105, 109

V

vibration
  of the Qutbiyyah, 36
  within the secret book, 72, 82

W

week, one—in the world, 56
Wisdom, seven levels of, 71–72,
  76, 81-82
witness, 97-102 *passim*
world
  destruction of the, 19–20
  never act for the, 99
worship, clarity in—of God, 108-
  110

Z

Zipporah ☺, 103–104

Publications

Books

Secrets of the Last Ant Man
Lailatul-Qadr: The Day of Light
Shaikh and Disciple
Islam, Jerusalem, and World Peace: Explanations of a Sufi
website: islamjerusalemandworldpeace.org
Prayer
Al-Asmā'ul-Husnā: The Duties and Qualities of Allāh
website: asmaulhusna.org
The Choice
Bawa Asks Bawa Muhaiyaddeen ☺ (Volumes One, Two, & Three)
Life Is a Dream: A Book of Sufi Verse
A Timeless Treasury of Sufi Quotations
The Four Virtues and Their Relationship
to Good Behavior and Bad Conduct
Sūratur-Rahmah: The Form of Compassion
God's Psychology: A Sufi Explanation
The Point Where God and Man Meet
The Map of the Journey to God: Lessons from the School of Grace
The Golden Words of a Sufi Sheikh, Revised Edition
A Book of God's Love
The Resonance of Allah: Resplendent Explanations Arising from
the *Nūr*, Allāh's Wisdom of Grace
The Tree That Fell to the West: Autobiography of a Sufi
Questions of Life — Answers of Wisdom (Volumes One & Two)
The Fast of Ramadan: The Inner Heart Blossoms
Hajj: The Inner Pilgrimage
The Triple Flame: The Inner Secrets of Sufism
A Song of Muhammad ☺
To Die Before Death: The Sufi Way of Life
A Mystical Journey
Why Can't I See the Angels: Children's Questions to a Sufi Saint
Treasures of the Heart: Sufi Stories for Young Children
Come to the Secret Garden: Sufi Tales of Wisdom
My Love You My Children: 101 Stories for Children of All Ages
Maya Veeram or The Forces of Illusion
God, His Prophets and His Children

Four Steps to Pure *Īmān*
The Wisdom of Man
Truth & Light: Brief Explanations
Songs of God's Grace
The Guidebook to the True Secret of the Heart (Volumes One & Two)
The Divine Luminous Wisdom That Dispels the Darkness
Wisdom of the Divine (Volumes One to Six)
The Tasty, Economical Cookbook, Second Edition

Booklets
Beyond Creation
Can We Ever Regain Our Innocence?
Come to Prayer: The Wake-up Song
Du'ā' Kanzul-'arsh (The Invocation of the Treasure of the Throne)
An Explanation of the Benefits of Reciting the *Salawāt*
The Foot of the Qutb ☺
The Hospital Story
King Solomon ☺ and the Fish & Explanations about Jinns and Fairies
The Opening of the Mosque of Shaikh M. R. Bawa Muhaiyaddeen ☺
Sindanay & I Will Tell You of the Way
Sufism
Why We Recite the Maulids

A Contemporary Sufi Speaks Series
On the Meaning of Fellowship
Mind, Desire, and the Billboards of the World
On Peace of Mind
On the Signs of Destruction
Teenagers and Parents
On the True Meaning of Sufism
On Unity: The Legacy of the Prophets

Gems of Wisdom series:
Vol. 1: The Value of Good Qualities
Vol. 2: Beyond Mind and Desire
Vol. 3: The Innermost Heart
Vol. 4: Come to Prayer

The Instructions
The Fox and the Crocodile and Do Not Carry Tales
God Is Very Light
Prayer: Starting Over
Unity

Pamphlets
Advice to Prisoners
Faith
The Golden Words of a Sufi Sheikh: Preface to the Book
Grieving for the Dead
Keep the Pond Clean
Letter to the World Family
Love Is the Remedy, God Is the Healer
Marriage
A Prayer for Father's Day
A Prayer for My Children
A Prayer from My Heart
Strive for a Good Life
Sufi: A Brief Explanation
A Sufi Perspective on Business
25 Duties—The True Meaning of Fellowship
Who Is God?
With Every Breath, Say Lā Ilāha Ill-Allāhu
Why Man Has No Peace (from My Love You My Children)
The Wisdom and Grace of the Sufis

Foreign Language Publications
Ein Zeitgenössischer Sufi Spricht über Inneren Frieden
Deux Discours tirés du Livre L'Islam et la Paix Mondiale:
Explications d'un Soufi
La Paix
Quién es Dios? Una Explicatión por el Sheikh Sufi

Other Publications
Bawa Muhaiyaddeen Fellowship Calendar
Morning *Dhikr*
at the Mosque of Shaikh M. R. Bawa Muhaiyaddeen ☺
Songs of Divine Wisdom
(a notated version of songs by M. R. Bawa Muhaiyaddeen ☺
The *Subhāna Maulid*

Contact Information

WE INVITE YOU TO VISIT

The Fellowship in Philadelphia, Pennsylvania, where Bawa Muhaiyaddeen ☺ stayed when he visited the United States, continues to serve as a meeting house and a reservoir of materials for everyone wishing access to his teachings.

The Mosque of Shaikh M. R. Bawa Muhaiyaddeen ☺ is located on the same property as the Fellowship. The five daily prayers and Friday congregational prayers are observed.

The Mazār, the resting place of Bawa Muhaiyaddeen ☺, is an hour west of the Fellowship and open daily between sunrise and sunset.

email: **info@bmf.org**
website: **www.bmf.org/publications**

TO LISTEN TO THE TEACHINGS

http://s3.nexuscast.com/start/bmfdd/
The Daily Discourse: the teachings of Bawa Muhaiyaddeen ☺ in chronological order, beginning every even hour on the hour, Eastern Time [GMT-5].

http://sc1.mystreamserver.com/start/bmfhs/
Live from the Fellowship House and Mosque: morning *dhikr*, five-times prayer, Bawa Muhaiyaddeen's discourses and songs, meetings, and special events.

http://s3.nexuscast.com/start/bmf786/
24/7 Radio: A continuous stream of over three hundred discourses and songs from the CD of the Month, updated every Anniversary Weekend.

Al-hamdu lillāh!
All praise is due to God!

www.ingramcontent.com/pod-product-compliance
Lightning Source LLC
Chambersburg PA
CBHW072155160426
43197CB00012B/2398